# SATURATE
# FIELD GUIDE

*Principles and Practices for*

## Being Disciples of Jesus
*in the*
## Everyday Stuff of Life

JEFF VANDERSTELT
& BEN CONNELLY

*Saturate Field Guide* by Jeff Vanderstelt and Ben Connelly



**Saturate**
227 Bellevue Way NE, #224
Bellevue, WA 98004



**Hardcover ISBN**: 0996849300
**Paperback ISBN**: 978-1-7324913-1-1
**eBook ISBN**: 0996849319

**Cover design** | Nick Osterman & Charlie Apel
**Editing** | Lisa Kukkamaa-Baker
**Book Design** | Charlie Apel

Printed in the USA | Third Printing

# PRAISE FOR SATURATE

*"I've always been grateful for Jeff Vanderstelt's heart for discipleship. Rather than drawing people to himself, he labors to help others understand the power they possess in the Spirit. He does what all good leaders should do: spends his days equipping others to do the work of the ministry."*

FRANCIS CHAN

NEW YORK TIMES BEST-SELLING AUTHOR, CRAZY LOVE AND FORGOTTEN GOD

---

*"I have known Jeff to faithfully live out the philosophies of life and day-to-day ministry contained in these pages, and have watched firsthand as God produced much fruit. I pray it encourages you."*

MATT CHANDLER

LEAD PASTOR, THE VILLAGE CHURCH, DALLAS, TEXAS; PRESIDENT, ACTS 29 CHURCH PLANTING NETWORK

---

*"If someone were to ask me where to go to learn about discipleship, I would hand them the Bible along with Jeff Vanderstelt's book Saturate. Readers will find themselves taking a survey of their lives, seeing the areas that God desires to take captive for his glory. Whether you are a preacher, homemaker, small-group leader, high school student, or new convert, Saturate will spur you on to live a life that will influence others to know Jesus while growing people in Jesus, not just at church, but in all of life."*

JACKIE HILL-PERRY

POET; WRITER; HIP-HOP ARTIST

*"This is a thought-provoking, heart-warming account of a body of believers taking God's call to live as family seriously. This book challenges and encourages all of us to intentionally live on mission in the mundane details and events of everyday life."*

STEVE TIMMIS

EXECUTIVE DIRECTOR, ACTS 29 CHURCH PLANTING NETWORK

---

*"Jeff Vanderstelt uses an ordinary experience to give us extraordinary insight into what it means to be a disciple of Jesus. Saturate is a great challenge to all of us to stop doing church and be the church!"*

DAVE FERGUSON

LEAD PASTOR, COMMUNITY CHRISTIAN CHURCH, NAPERVILLE, ILLINOIS; LEAD VISIONARY, NEWTHING

---

*"Whether you are new to the faith or a seasoned believer, Jeff's words will encourage you and focus God's gospel on every facet of your life. This book will challenge the way you see your Savior, your mission, and your everyday life."*

ED STETZER

PRESIDENT, LIFEWAY RESEARCH; AUTHOR, SUBVERSIVE KINGDOM; WWW.EDSTETZER.COM

This nine-part video series enhances and deepens the learning experience for groups using the Saturate Field Guide. Week by week, Jeff Vanderstelt articulates and summarizes key ideas, themes, and principles as groups engage and process the Field Guide together. Additional concepts and training will enhance learning for groups as they move toward becoming a community centered on the gospel and on the mission of Jesus.

## VIDEOS TO ENHANCE YOUR WEEKLY LEARNING:

| | |
|---|---|
| INTRO | **What is Gospel Saturation?** |
| WEEK 1 | **Jesus is Better** |
| WEEK 2 | **All of Life Discipleship** |
| WEEK 3 | **Identity of Family** |
| WEEK 4 | **Identity of Servant** |
| WEEK 5 | **Identity of Missionary** |
| WEEK 6 | **Rhythms Part One (Eat, Celebrate, Recreate)** |
| WEEK 7 | **Rhythms Part Two (Listen, Story, Bless)** |
| WEEK 8 | **Commissioned Together** |

**EXTRAS:**
- **Equipping the Church: What is APEST?**
- **Leader Video**

**saturatetheworld.com/fg**

**Use code "sfgv20" to receive a 20% discount.**

# Appendix Resources

The Appendix to this book, along with additional resources and videos, are all available at:

***saturatetheworld.com/fg***

---

**Appendix A:**
Telling Your Gospel Story

**Appendices B & C:**
Missional Community Covenant Template & Sample

**Appendix D:**
Alternative 16-Week Schedule

# contents

For the earth will be filled with the knowledge of the glory of the Lord as the waters cover the sea.

---

HABAKKUK 2:14

Blessed are those who hear the word of God and obey it.

Jesus of Nazareth

LUKE 11:28 (NIV)

# a note of thanks

We're honored that you picked up this Saturate resource. Our deepest hope is that you find it useful in your pursuit of living as a disciple of Jesus, and our prayer is that God will use our humble efforts to produce great fruit in and through your life.

These first two sections provide a vital foundation for your upcoming eight-week journey, especially if it's a journey you're taking with others (which for many reasons, both theological and practical, we hope that it is).

Enjoy the coming weeks of growing together, and may God's grace be evident as you join many across the world in pursuing God's vision of "Jesus saturation," by His power and for His glory.

**Jeff Vanderstelt & Ben Connelly**

# BEFORE YOUR FIRST MEETING

## INTRODUCTION

In the Old Testament book of Habakkuk, God gives a big vision: "For the earth will be filled with the knowledge of the glory of the Lord as the waters cover the sea."[1] That's a picture of saturation. God is accomplishing this vision through his Son, Jesus Christ, working through his body, the church. Ephesians 1:22-23 says, "He put all things under his feet and gave him as head over all things to the Church, which is his body, the fullness of him who fills all in all." Jesus is the head of his body, the Church, through which he intends to fill every place with his presence. This is saturation—Jesus saturation.

God's mission is that his people will be so saturated in Jesus that every person, in every place, would daily experience the good news of Jesus and be transformed by it in the course of their daily lives. Can you imagine every city, neighborhood, school, extracurricular activity, office, retail center, and industrial hub proclaiming the glory of Jesus in words and gracious deeds?

| JESUS SATURATION |
| --- |
| every person (man, woman, and child) |
| in every place having a daily encounter with Jesus |
| in words spoken and deeds done through his people. |

For video and additional resources pertaining to the Intro, visit:

www.saturatetheworld.com/fg/intro

This is God's intention for his world and he wants you to be a part of it! And, amazingly enough, if you know, trust, love, and follow Jesus, you already are! Yes, you, the unimpressive and average Jesus follower, have been entrusted by God with his mission of saturating the world with his glory through the everyday stuff of life. (If you haven't yet submitted your life to Jesus, we pray you will. Jesus saturation can't happen through you until you have.)

1. Habakkuk 2:14

It has always been God's intention to choose normal, everyday people to demonstrate his amazing power and glory. The Bible is filled with story after story of such people. He's not looking for the most impressive person because he already is that person.

## WHO IS THIS FIELD GUIDE FOR?

Why should you devote so much time and effort to this idea of "Jesus saturation"? Because you're a perfect candidate for God to use to accomplish his purpose! But in our experience, we all need a little help understanding and pursuing God's purpose. This resource is intended to give you that help.

Maybe you're just considering who Jesus is and what he claims to do. The interactive nature of this Field Guide, and the community who will surround you as you work through it, will help you wrestle with the concepts that followers of Jesus (disciples) claim to be true.

Maybe you're a new follower of Jesus, or are new to the idea that discipleship and mission are 24/7 realities, rather than merely occurring a couple hours each Sunday. Over the coming weeks, you'll not only learn about all-of-life discipleship, but gain experience with it.

Maybe you've been a follower of Jesus for a long while, but like many of us, have a hard time translating the truths you believe in your mind to the reality of your everyday life. The questions, activities, prayers, and exercises in the coming pages will prompt you to do exactly that—to put your thoughts and theology into hands-on practice.

In short, every follower of Jesus needs help translating our belief in the gospel (we'll define "gospel" in Week One, Day One) into action and fruit. And given our tendency to wander away from God, we then need help keeping that gospel at the center of our action. This Field Guide is intended to help with all of this, because it is all necessary to be holistic disciples of Jesus, in the everyday stuff of life.

## GOD'S CALLING TO ISRAEL

This isn't a new idea. God called his people Israel to remember him and show the world what he was like through the everyday stuff, the big and the small. The special feasts, which were extraordinary, were meant to remind them that everyday meals mattered as well. Parties are God's idea. During the Israelites' parties and feasts, they were to remind one another that all of life was to be done as an expression of their love for God. God called them to see their celebrations and feasts as an expression of their worship. He wanted them to use something mundane and everyday—eating—as a reminder that he is to be the center of all the everyday stuff. God is brilliant, isn't he?

He wants us to see that all of life, every aspect of it, is a good gift from him. He wants our hearts to cry out, "God is so good!" in the middle of everyday life. He wants us to eat, play, create, work, celebrate, rest, and relate to one another for his glory. God always intended that every part of life be a participation in his activity in the world and a celebration of his goodness to us all. So he told Israel to do all the stuff of life—working, resting, eating, and celebrating—in remembrance of him. I love this about God!

The Israelites forgot who they were and why they had been called to be God's people. Their feasts became empty, heartless, ritualistic events. They were partying without the life of the party, celebrating without a reason to celebrate. That led to self-absorbed consumption and heartless activities without love. The same can happen to us if we forget to keep God central. Church becomes an empty, heartless, religious event.

## JESUS DID WHAT ISRAEL COULD NOT

So Jesus came as God in the flesh to show us the heart of God for people. Before Jesus did any formal ministry, he spent thirty years of his life doing normal, mundane, unremarkable stuff. He lived a regular life for the glory of God. He ate, played, learned, celebrated, worked with his hands, and rested just like the rest of humanity. Think about this! God moved into the neighborhood, and nobody but a few shepherds took notice. And they did so only because a bunch of angels showed up while they were watching their sheep and told them to go see Jesus.

Jesus lived a normal, quiet life for thirty years in an unknown town. He was so normal that when he began his public ministry, the people from his hometown couldn't believe it. "Isn't this Jesus of Nazareth?" they asked. "Isn't he the carpenter's son who lived among us, doing normal stuff like the rest of us?" (see Matt. 13:53-58). The difference is that Jesus did everything for his heavenly Father's glory. He lived all of his life as an expression of his love for God the Father. Jesus did what Israel didn't do. He did what we don't do. He set apart every aspect of life as holy unto God.

Jesus was set apart for God in the world, and everything he did was to glorify God. He was holy, and every aspect of his life was holy, because he did it unto God. When he ate, he blessed God for good provision. When he worked, he knew he was doing it unto God and showing off the creativity of our Creator. He submitted to authority humbly and gladly as an act of submission to God, who ordains rulers in every place. He served, shared with, and loved others because he knew God is a serving God who gives good gifts and is love himself. Jesus lived every part of his life in submission to God. Every action was an act of love to God and others, and every one of his thoughts was directed by God. Jesus lived a fully God-dependent life. Holy Jesus lived a holy life wholly unto God.

Finally, after thirty years of quiet, submissive, humble worship, Jesus began to publicly proclaim the good news of God's kingdom—that there was a new order to things, and he was going to bring all of life under God's authority. He wanted a holy people who would live all of life wholly unto God. God was making a way for all of life to be restored to the way he always intended it to be. Everything could be made good and all of life could be worship. Life could be as it was always meant to be!

But Jesus didn't just proclaim the good news. He lived a good-news life, showing what God's rule and reign looks like when God breaks into the normal stuff of everyday life.

## A NEW VIEW OF CHURCH: GOD'S DISCIPLES IN THE EVERYDAY STUFF OF LIFE

Jesus did this so that we also could do this. He came to rescue a people back to God so all of life would be seen as sacred, all of life would be set apart unto God, and everyday stuff would be seen as worship.

Look at the picture to the right. Some people think church is a building you go to. Others think it's the programs and events that happen there [the circles inside the building, representing activities], while others think it's mainly the leaders who run those events [the stick figures inside the building]. They think the job of those leaders is to get people to invite their friends to the building [the stick figures and arrows pointing toward the building]. They also encourage people to give their time [the clock], their money [the dollar sign], and their skills and gifts [the gift-wrapped present] to support what happens primarily in the building.

But though we might gather together in a building, the church of Jesus is the people of God saved through the person and work of Jesus Christ for his purposes in the world. God's intent was never to have us define church merely as an event on Sunday. We don't go to church. We are the Church sent out into the world [that's why there are arrows going out of the building].

Jesus wants us to live all of life fully for his glory in the world—every part and every person. Jesus didn't live, serve, suffer, and die so we could just attend a Christian event. He lived and died so we could become his people who are sent into every part of the world on his behalf. He wants all people everywhere to see and know about him, and he wants everyone to know that everything is to be done for his glory. We now see our time, our money, and our unique abilities as means to serve both the people who are the church and those in our cities who don't know the great news of God's love for them in Jesus Christ. All of life counts and everyone matters.

Many followers of Jesus wrongly believe that God's work is mainly done in a church building by a few paid professionals, and that the members of the church are primarily needed to volunteer to run the programs and provide the financial support. Normal stuff doesn't count, because God doesn't work in the normal stuff, they believe. They can't imagine themselves on his mission in the world, because they have wrongly believed God's mission isn't in the world. Church seems so disconnected from the rest of their lives. Clearly, God can't use them, and therefore he must not want them.

But this is simply not true. God loves to use normal people in the everyday stuff of life. He wants everyone involved in all of life.

## HOW DO WE USE THIS FIELD GUIDE?

What you're currently reading is a Field Guide. It's not a book; books are generally designed to give information and to be read cover to cover, often in just a few days. While the content here accompanies a book — Jeff Vanderstelt's *Saturate: Being Disciples of Jesus in the Everyday Stuff of Life* (Crossway, 2015)[2] — the Field Guide can also be an independent resource, and is crafted with completely different purposes in mind:

1. Instead of simply providing information, the Field Guide gives you principles and practice, helping you apply the information and obey God's words. Instead of merely asking you to read it in its entirety in a short time, the Field Guide asks you to bite off a small piece every day for eight weeks and to interact with the content each day.

2. Over the coming weeks, you'll marinate on Scripture, immerse yourself in prayer, dive deep into introspection, carry out practical exercises, discuss and debate, make plans, and more. And ideally, you'll do all of this alongside a group of individuals who are likewise interacting with the content each day.

3. As mentioned, we highly recommend working through the coming weeks in a group. While there's no magic number or composition of the group, we suggest about six to twelve people. We encourage each week's meeting start by sharing good food and drink together and simply spending some time enjoying one another, in addition to discussing the previous week's content. Another idea we suggest for your weekly meeting is to begin by someone sharing their story[3], then receiving encouragement and prayer from the rest of the community. See Appendix A for some suggestions on sharing your story with others.

---

2. Content from *Saturate* is summarized in each week's activities, and each week indicates corresponding chapters in *Saturate*

3. Every person has a story to tell. Whether the story of their day or the story of their life. Often we're telling a story of who we are, what has been broken in our lives (past and present), how was it mended (or how we look for it be fixed), what life currently looks like, and our hopes and dreams for where we're headed.

Beyond that, the only rules for forming your group are: Ensuring that those involved ...

**A.** ... are willing to speak honestly about concepts that excite them, make them nervous, are difficult, and are willing to both give and receive "truth in love" (Eph. 4:15-16) from the group—of course, it's okay if this is hard at times; following Jesus often is!

**B.** ... can commit the time to complete the weekly rhythm listed below and attend a weekly meal together, a "family meal" where you'll meet to discuss how God is training you, individually and together.

**4.** Establish your weekly rhythm. After your initial meeting, you'll launch into a regular "rhythm" together for the next eight weeks (If you're newer to Missional Community theory and practice, or if you or others in your group would have a difficult time committing to the daily work, you might consider splitting each week of the Field Guide into two weeks[4]). Starting in Week One, there are seven distinct daily activities for you to work through, all centered around one weekly theme. While a little extra time wouldn't hurt, Days One through Five of each week can generally be completed in about 30 minutes each day:

**Day 1: Start**—a brief overview of that week's theme, including summaries and quotes from corresponding sections of *Saturate*, followed by a few reflection questions to get your mind going for the week

- **Day 2: Read**—a few biblical passages to read and mark up, followed by questions to answer, to help you form a healthy biblical view of that week's theme
- **Day 3: Think**—introspective questions and activities to help you see how your mind and life currently display an understanding and application of that week's theme
- **Day 4: Pray**—guided prayer exercises which ask for the Spirit's help in that week's theme and thank God for his grace in our weakness
- **Day 5: Do**—a few action items, case studies, and/or activities to help you put that week's theme into practice, and to help you define and develop areas of growth
- **Day 6: Meet**—based on the preparation and experience of each week, this day guides your "family



4. For an Alternative 16-Week Schedule that may suit you and your Missional Community better, see Appendix D

meal," with questions and exercises to discuss with the community walking through the Field Guide together

- **Day 7: Floating Day of Rest**[5]—this weekly "day off" encourages readers to rest and celebrate God's goodness (or to catch up!), before wrapping up each week's theme

5. Finally, as we acknowledge the reality of our busy lives, we encourage you to hold in tension during the next eight weeks that:

   **A.** The Field Guide works best if you try to diligently carry out each day's activity. Of course you may miss a day here or there, but if you just breeze through the written portions without stopping to consider the more practical elements, you've missed the benefit of its design.

   **B.** Having said that, if you do miss a day—occasionally!—don't stress out. In our experience, we've learned that it will likely serve you better to give the day you missed a quick glance, to skip it altogether, or to revisit it on a "Rest Day," than to try to make it up and cram two (or more) full days in the next time you pick up the Field Guide. Again, the greatest benefit of the coming weeks comes if you're consistent and committed to the whole process.

## THE VISION FOR ALL GOD'S PEOPLE ... INCLUDING YOU!

In Ephesians 1:23, the apostle Paul calls the church Jesus's body (his sōma), through which he fills all in all. Paul's vision, given to him by the Holy Spirit, was of the church being the body of Christ, through which Jesus fills every place with his presence through his people.

All God's people, everywhere, filling everyday life with his presence.

That's the vision of *Saturate*. And that's what we hope to help you step into, alongside many people, throughout history and across the world, as you work through this Field Guide.

If you're ready to be better equipped for the life of discipleship God has called you to, then pause and pray for his help for the coming weeks, then look through the questions in the next section, and head to your group's initial meeting where you'll jump right in!

5. We recommend that your community agree together on the day you'll make each week's Day of Rest—maybe a weekend

## QUESTIONS TO CONSIDER BEFORE YOUR FIRST MEETING

Having read this introduction, here are some questions to consider personally which will serve as a guide for your initial group meeting.

1. As you read this introduction, what's your initial impression? What's new or exciting to you? What makes you nervous or hesitant? What are you confused by, and what do you have questions about?

2. Several views of "the church" were described in the previous pages and are summarized to the right. Think about which one you are most familiar with. Then in the space below describe where you learned about what "the church" is and what your understanding is based on (for example social/family norms, biblical teaching, experience, etc.). Has your definition changed over time? Is there anything here you find challenging or new?

Church is primarily a building I go to.

Church is primarily the programs and events that happen in and around that building, or are sponsored by the Church.

Church is primarily the leaders who run the events, who get people to invite friends to the events, and who encourage people to give their time, money, skills, and gifts to support the programs and events.

Church is primarily the people of God saved through the person and work of Jesus Christ for his purposes in the world.

**3.** How do you define discipleship? Has your understanding of living as a disciple changed over time? (Note: We'll discuss discipleship in Week 2.)

**4.** Have you ever considered that the normal stuff of everyday life—our meals, jobs, homes, free time, relationships—are all areas of discipleship? That everything we do can be done "to the glory of God"? Why or why not?

**5.** Do you think there are things that you've done, conversations you've had that are likely "discipleship," "ministry," or "living as God's church," even though they were never labeled as such or validated as such because they didn't fit an event or program? What are some examples of these?

**6.** Do you have any confusion about how the coming weeks will work? How are you feeling about the journey you're starting?

**7.** Would you consider being the first one to share your story at the initial meeting? What would make you eager to share? What would make you hesitant? (For more detail on what this entails, see the "Sharing Stories" section in the coming pages' "Suggested Outline for Your First Meeting.")

# SUGGESTED OUTLINE FOR YOUR FIRST MEETING

INTRODUCTION

## EAT, DRINK & BE MERRY

For the initial meeting, it may be helpful for someone (the host, the people who called the group together, or someone else) to provide a meal, or at least snacks and drinks, for the community—and to provide childcare if needed. During this initial meeting, you'll make a plan together to take care of food and kids during the upcoming meetings.

## DISCUSSION

Based on the material covered so far, honestly discuss these questions with your faith community. Boldly speak truth in love to, and humbly hear truth in love from, each other. Encourage, exhort, commit to help, celebrate, and even rebuke each other in these areas.

1. Has everyone read up to and through this section? Assuming yes, what stood out to you? What was new? What was exciting or hopeful? What was difficult?

2. Was there anything that raised questions or confusion?

3. From the "Questions to Consider," what has been your view of the church? Where did it come from? Do you feel you need to expand your view of the church?

4. From the "Questions to Consider," what stuck out to you as you considered discipleship, the stuff of everyday life, and things you've done that might not automatically be labeled "ministry"?

The next questions are the most logistical in the entire Field Guide. They're important as you begin this journey together, to make sure everyone is on the same page. Consider each question through the lens of "discipleship together"—how would you discuss each if those around you were an actual, healthy, nuclear family?

**5.** Do we have a weekly time and place we can all commit to meet for a couple hours, share a family meal, and discuss each week's theme?

We will commit to the: ☐ 8-Week Schedule ☐ 16-Week Schedule

We'll meet on:
Each week's floating "Day of Rest" is a day you choose to rest and recreate (or catch up!).

| | day | AM<br>PM | time | | place |
|---|---|---|---|---|---|

Do we want to commit to a shared day? If so, is there a day each week that makes the most sense?

Once you've established your meeting day and "Day of Rest," each week's weekly rhythm should start the day after your weekly family meal.

| Our weekly rhythm, "Day One", will begin on: | | day |
|---|---|---|

**6.** Will we all commit to fully giving ourselves to the weekly rhythm of prep work and family meals, and can we agree to be honest and open with each other—even when things aren't always easy or comfortable? If there's anything that makes it hard for anyone to say "yes," work through that as a community, humbly speaking truth in love to each other.

**7.** As a community, how can we best serve each other as we work through each day's activities? (For example, do verbal processors need to walk through each day together? What accountability might we need, at least during the first couple weeks, to stay on target?)

**8.** One recommendation is sharing a meal together during each week's meeting. How will our community carry this out? (For example: will the host provide? Will we all claim a week or two and rotate bringing food? Will we do themed potlucks?)

**9.** How do we want to take care of children during our weekly family meals? (For example: do we hire babysitters—if so, do we all pitch in for the cost, or just parents? Do we rotate watching kids? Will they stay with us—for dinner or for the whole meeting?)

## SHARING STORIES

A key element of discipleship together is knowing each other well. Every week, one or two of us will share our stories. The goal in sharing stories is to listen for things to celebrate and thank God for, and to listen for themes or areas of life to ask questions and speak truth in love, as we point each other toward Jesus. Our stories simply recap our lives and how God has shaped us to this point. They should take 10–15 minutes to share, and can cover things like:

- Seasons (the general flow of your life—such as childhood, school, marriage, parenting, empty-nest, places you've lived, jobs you've had, schools you've attended)
- High and low points (key moments/experiences that have shaped you)
- Relationships (key people who have shaped you in different seasons)
- Faith (your journey [for better or worse!], consistent struggles, areas to celebrate)

Invite someone to share, then as you wrap up this initial meeting, take time to pray intentionally for the person who shared and ask who will share next week.

⊙ *Visit Appendix A, "Telling Your Gospel Story," for more information.*

WEEK 1

# Jesus

# START

## WEEK 1, DAY 1

*Prayerfully and thoughtfully read this week's reading below (or read chapters 3-6 of Saturate). As you read, circle, underline, write in the margins, and interact with concepts or ideas that are new, difficult, inspiring, etc.*

For video and additional resources pertaining to Week 1, visit:

www.saturatetheworld.com/fg/week1

"Gospel" is an overused word in the Church today. It's come to mean everything in some circles, and nothing in others. But whether you're a follower of Jesus or not, and no matter how long you have been if you are, Jesus is at the heart of the gospel, and the gospel is at the heart of following Jesus.

### THE *WHOLE* GOSPEL

The great apostle Paul wrote to the first-Century church at Corinth that he "delivered to you *as of first importance* what I also received: that Christ died for our sins in accordance with the Scriptures, that he was buried, that he was raised on the third day in accordance with the Scriptures" (1 Corinthians 15:3-4). This is the gospel; it's the culmination of the great story of redemption God has been unfolding since before time began. Every one of us is a participant somewhere in his storyline of redemption.

Paul reminded the church in Rome of the confidence we can have in Jesus and his work. In Romans 1:16-17, he writes: "For I am not ashamed of the gospel, for it is the power of God for salvation to everyone who believes, to the Jew first and also to the Greek. For in it the righteousness of God is revealed from faith for faith, as it is written, 'The righteous shall live by faith.'"

On one hand, the gospel is "the power of God for salvation." Salvation from what? What do we need to be saved from? God wants to save us from the penalty of sin—salvation from what we've done; the power of sin—salvation for what we're called to do today; and the presence of sin—salvation for our future...

On the other hand, in saying "the righteous shall live by faith," Paul is saying, in essence, that the good news is that God has power to save everyone who walks by faith, believing God can save him or her. The good news is that God saves us as we trust in him and not in ourselves. And the means by which God does this—the righteousness that is revealed—is the life, death, and resurrection of Jesus applied to our lives by God's Spirit.

Followers of Jesus must see all of life—our lives and others'—through the lens of the gospel story. And to do so, we must understand the whole gospel. That is, the power of God for salvation through faith in the person and work of Jesus Christ, for the purpose of glorifying God and participating in his mission of saturation, by the power of the Holy Spirit to make disciples who make disciples. In a right understanding, the gospel has past, present, and future implications. This week, we're considering who Jesus is and all he has done, is doing, and will do for us.

## JESUS DID IT BETTER: WE *HAVE BEEN* SAVED

In Romans 3:23, Paul tells us, "For all have sinned and fall short of the glory of God." To sin is to think, believe, or act in any way that is not like God or in submission to what God commands. We all have fallen short; every one of us has sinned. And "the wages of sin is death" (Rom. 6:23a). The result of our sin is damage to ourselves, brokenness in our relationships, destruction to the world around us, death to our physical bodies, and, ultimately, an eternal spiritual death, separation forever from a relationship with God, the giver and sustainer of life. Our rebellion, our sin, leads to brokenness...

"But the free gift of God is eternal life in Christ Jesus our Lord" (Rom. 6:23b). God has made a way to give us something different from what we deserve. Since no natural human being ever has lived or ever will live a life perfectly glorifying to God, Jesus came and took on flesh as the God-man. Jesus became for humanity the true and better human, the true Son of Man and Son of God. He submitted himself perfectly to God the Father. He obeyed him in everything, doing only what God the Father told him to do. This perfect obedience—this perfect life—has been given to us. Jesus is the gift of God to humanity (John 3:16). This is good news!

By faith in Jesus, you and I are saved from the need to live a perfect life to gain God's approval. Paul says that our lives are now hidden with Christ in God (Col. 3:3). That means that if, by faith, you have trusted Jesus as the One who perfectly obeyed God on your behalf, God sees Jesus's performance as yours. He accepts you because of Jesus.

## JESUS DOES IT BETTER: WE *ARE BEING* SAVED

The first-century church at Corinth had begun to question whether there was a bodily resurrection from the dead—whether people will be given new bodies to live in in a new world one day. This was huge! If people are not raised from the dead and given new bodies, then what happened with Jesus? Paul tells them our entire faith is futile if there is no resurrection (1 Cor. 15:12-19).

Paul confronted their wrong thinking by reminding them of the gospel: "Now I would remind you, brothers, of the gospel I preached to you, which you received, in which you stand, and by which you are being saved, if you hold fast to the word I preached to you—unless you believed in vain. For I delivered to you as of first importance what I also received: that Christ died for our sins in accordance with the Scriptures, that he was buried, that he was raised on the third day in accordance with the Scriptures, and that he appeared to Cephas, then to the twelve" (1 Cor. 15:1-5).

If we have faith in Jesus to save us, we have been saved and we are being saved.

Paul uses the language of being saved in describing what the gospel is still doing. Yes, the gospel is good news about a past event—Jesus lived and died in a definite time in history to forgive us of our sins. Yet the gospel is also good news about what God continues to do in us and through us. Jesus was raised from the dead on the third day. He is alive! He lives for us, and by his Spirit, he lives in us and works through us.

Most followers of Jesus believe that one day, we will be like him (1 John 3:2) and will live in a perfect world with him. But many forget that in the present, he comes into our lives by his Spirit to give us a glimpse, a foretaste, of the future so that we will live differently today. As we trust and depend on him to work in us, he enables us to live the new and better life now.

## JESUS WILL MAKE IT BETTER: WE *WILL BE* SAVED

What you love most, you also fear losing the most. And whatever threatens what you love most controls you. We love God because he first loved us. He loved us by sending the Son to satisfy his just wrath against us for our sin. So we have no need to fear judgment coming against us for our sin. Perfect love casts out fear (1 John 4:7-21).

First Peter 1:3-5 tells us that God "has caused us to be born again to a living hope through the resurrection of Jesus Christ from the dead, to an inheritance that is imperishable, undefiled, and unfading, kept in heaven for you, who by God's power are being guarded through faith for a salvation ready to be revealed in the last time." Not only do we have no need to be afraid of future judgment if our faith is in Jesus, but we also have no need to fear loss. Our salvation is kept in heaven for us. Also, Jesus is presently at the right hand of God the Father, representing all those who have faith in him. He is securing us until the end. And he has all authority in heaven and on earth (Matt. 28:18). The thing that matters most cannot be taken away from us, and nothing can happen to us to prevent us from inheriting it.

Our relationship with God, our future salvation, and our hope to live eternally with Jesus on a new earth are already secured. If our faith is in

Jesus to save us, we have been saved, we are being saved, and we will be saved.

Scripture also tells us that in the future, God will make all things new. All sin will be eradicated. All that is broken will be restored. Every person who belongs to Jesus will be healed. All relationships will be reconciled. We will enjoy a perfect world with Jesus at the center forever. It will be stunningly amazing! Jesus doesn't just hold and secure our future. He gives us a perfectly new one as well.

## THE GOSPEL IS THE KEY

As we'll see throughout this Field Guide, believing these truths makes all the difference in the world. Everything else this week—and in the coming weeks—begins and ends with Jesus: who he is and all he does in the gospel. Without him, we're helpless and hopeless; we seek someone or something else to give us hope and joy; we rely on our power (or lack thereof) for faith and strength; we fear other things, which can then control our lives. Bottom line, *you need to believe the gospel in order to step out and obey Jesus.*

*You need to believe he has saved you. You are forgiven and loved; there is no record of wrongs against you.*

*You need to believe he is saving you. You can do all things through Christ who gives you strength.*

*You need to believe he will save you. You have nothing to fear because your future is in his hands.*

---

## DAY 1: QUESTIONS TO CONSIDER

1. Do you believe—or live as if —you have to perform well for God in order to receive his loving acceptance? Do you believe God loves you more when you obey and less when you disobey? If so, how can this be understood as disbelief in what Jesus has *already* done?

Sometimes. I know God's love for me never changes but there's a part of me that always wants to be faithful to him. This can become disbelief when my focus becomes about my faithfulness, not his. Even more, it shows up as unbelief when I feel I haven't done enough to see goodness from God.

2. Do you believe—or live as if—your holiness is enabled by your own power and strength? Do you truly believe the Spirit of God is alive and living in you today, who alone has the ability to work in and through you? If not, how can this be understood as disbelief in what Jesus is *currently* doing?

Thankfully, no. Even in my sin, I know my holiness comes from God. It is too good to be by my strength. Christ makes me holy.

3. Do you believe—or live as if—the future is unsure (even paralyzing)? Do you truly believe that eternity has been secured for you, by the death and resurrection of Jesus? If not, how can this be understood as disbelief in what Jesus *has promised* to do?

I believe my eternity is secure. The future doesn't always feel secure though. God is sovereign over the future but I tend to become indifferent when I "have no control".

4. Think about the phrases "we have been saved," "we are being saved," and "we will be saved." If all of these are true because of who Jesus is and what he's done, how should this impact our daily lives?

Every facet of my life should call on Jesus and praise His name. Especially in the little things that appear without meaning.

# READ

## WEEK 1, DAY 2

Prayerfully and thoughtfully read the biblical texts below, then spend a few moments reflecting on the truths therein by answering the questions at the end.

As you read, where do you see this week's three truths—Jesus's past, present, and future work in us and through us—in the following verses, whether explicitly mentioned, implied by actions, or as simply necessary to rightly understand the passage?

- ◻ Box areas you see Jesus's past work
- ○ Circle areas you see Jesus's ongoing work in peoples' lives
- ★ Star areas you see Jesus's future work

### JOHN 15:1-5

"I am the true vine, and my Father is the vinedresser. Every branch in me that does not bear fruit he takes away, and every branch that does bear fruit he prunes, that it may bear more fruit. Already you are clean because of the word that I have spoken to you. Abide in me, and I in you. As the branch cannot bear fruit by itself, unless it abides in the vine, neither can you, unless you abide in me. I am the vine; you are the branches. Whoever abides in me and I in him, he it is that bears much fruit, for apart from me you can do nothing."

### ROMANS 6:5-11, 23

For if we have been united with him in a death like his, we shall certainly be united with him in a resurrection like his. We know that our old self was crucified with him in order that the body of sin might be brought to nothing, so that we would no longer be enslaved to sin. For one who has died has been set free from sin. Now if we have died with Christ, we believe that we will also live with him. We know that Christ, being raised from the dead, will never die again; death no longer has dominion over him. For the death he died he died to sin, once for all, but the life he lives he lives to God. So you also must consider yourselves dead to sin and alive to God in Christ Jesus... For the wages of sin is death, but the free gift of God is eternal life in Christ Jesus our Lord.

### COLOSSIANS 1:16-20

For by him all things were created, in heaven and on earth, visible and invisible, whether thrones or dominions or rulers or authorities—all things were created through him and for him. And he is before all things, and in him all things hold together. And he is the head of the body, the church. He is the beginning, the firstborn from the dead, that in everything he might be preeminent. For in him all the fullness of God was pleased to dwell, and through him to reconcile to himself all things, whether on earth or in heaven, making peace by the blood of his cross.

### 1 CORINTHIANS 1:30-31

And because of him you are in Christ Jesus, who became to us wisdom from God, righteousness and sanctification and redemption, so that, as it is written, "Let the one who boasts, boast in the Lord."

### 2 CORINTHIANS 5:17-21

Therefore, if anyone is in Christ, he is a new creation; the old has gone, the new has come! All this is from God, who reconciled us to himself through Christ and gave us the ministry of reconciliation: that God was reconciling the world to himself in Christ, not counting men's sins against them. And he has committed to us the message of reconciliation. Therefore, we are ambassadors for Christ, God making his appeal through us. We implore you on behalf of Christ, be reconciled to God. For our sake he made him to be sin who knew no sin, so that in him we might become the righteousness of God.

### 1 PETER 1:3-5

Blessed be the God and Father of our Lord Jesus Christ! According to his great mercy, he has caused us to be born again to a living hope through the resurrection of Jesus Christ from the dead, to an inheritance that is imperishable, undefiled, and unfading, kept in heaven for you, who by God's power are being guarded through faith for a salvation ready to be revealed in the last time.

---

**FOR MORE:**

Romans 1:16-17 / 1 Corinthians 15:1-2 / 1 Peter 2:9-12 / Ephesians 2:8-10 / Philippians 2:12-13 / Galatians 2:20

## DAY 2: QUESTIONS TO CONSIDER

Answer these questions as you think about what you saw in today's verses:

1. What themes jumped out to you as you read these texts?

God has brought me to himself through Christ and is looking to do the same through me for others.

2. Look back through these verses: what personal struggles or beliefs are necessarily proven false if God's promises in these verses are true? (For example: if it's God who "wills and works for his good pleasure" in me [Philippians 2], then I don't have to—and indeed, I can't!—rely on myself to earn God's pleasure. Or [from 1 Corinthians 1], if God is the only reality we have to boast about, then what other sources of boasting in your life needs to stop?)

3. Which promise is hardest for you to believe or live out: that you have been saved, that you are being saved, or that you will be saved? Why?

There are plenty of stories, verses, and instances in the Bible where God's people didn't rest in the truths of the gospel. Think about what you know of the Bible and Story of God and answer the following questions. If you need a jumpstart, consider these passages: Genesis 3; Exodus 17; Romans 1:16-32; Galatians 1:8-11; Galatians 3.

**4.** What are examples of God's people not believing that God had saved them through Jesus? What did that disbelief lead them to do/think/say?

**5.** What are examples of God's people not relying on God's ongoing work in their lives? What did that disbelief lead them to do/think/say?

**6.** What are examples of God's people not trusting in God's future salvation and promise? What did that disbelief lead them to do/think/say?

# THINK

## WEEK 1, DAY 3

*Each week of this Field Guide builds on previous weeks. To prepare well for coming weeks, prayerfully and honestly work through these questions and exercises, in light of this week's themes.*

If the gospel is the core of everything we think, say, and do, then that means nothing else can be. We cannot be our own saviors.

Our job is not to be Jesus. Our job is to believe Jesus, depend on Jesus, and submit to Jesus working in and through us to accomplish his work. We are not meant to carry the weight of the world and the mission of Jesus on our shoulders. Jesus came to seek and save. He doesn't expect us to become the saviors.

Likewise, no other person or thing can be our savior: no job, no spouse, no boss, no child, no food or drink, no game, no school ... nothing can do what Jesus has done, is doing, and will do.

In Romans 1, Paul describes how we all exchange the truth of God for a lie and exchange worship of the Creator for worship of his creation. As a result, our minds become foolish and our hearts become dark. God turns us over to our worship of false gods, but they don't give us what we really want and need. So we lust for more. We want them to do what they can't really do for us, so we demand more from them. This lust is at the heart of all addiction. It's at the heart of all of our brokenness. We've all done it and we still do it.

In other words, we take a good thing and demand that it be a "god thing" for us. We do this with sex, friendships, food, alcohol, work, and even our children and spouses. Then, when God gives us over to our passions, we pervert or try to control our "god," twisting it, distorting it, and ultimately destroying what it was meant to be for us. God lets our sin and idolatry have its final way with us, so that our minds become twisted and we think, believe, and do all kinds of destructive things—tearing ourselves and others down (Rom. 1:18-31).

God lets us have life with the god we think will save us or save others, and it always fails. He wants us to know that no other person or thing can be God for us as he can, and no other person or thing can save as he does.

## DAY 3: QUESTIONS TO CONSIDER

Think about how these truths play out in your mind and life, by asking yourself the following questions in light of this week's focus on Jesus and the whole gospel. Don't feel like you need to answer every question. Instead, choose those that most resonate with you, that you feel God the Spirit speaking to you through, or maybe those that are most challenging to you—either way, we encourage you to answer at least one question from each section, and to write down your answers.

### WE *HAVE BEEN* SAVED

1. What are you tempted to hide or cover up? From whom do you strive to gain approval or acceptance? (Yourself? Someone else? God?) By doing so, where are you placing your identity? Where does God tell you your identity is truly found?

2. Are you living with regret, guilt, shame, or self-hatred for things you've done in the past? What does God tell you about your sin and any guilt and shame? What does it mean that he's already removed all the guilt from your life? If you're burdened by the past, who/what are you relying on for your functional salvation?

### WE *ARE BEING* SAVED

3. In what ways do you try to become holy by your own strength, actions, or disciplines? How often does that work? By doing so, where are you placing your hope?

4. What does it mean that God has given you his Spirit, who is the very power of God and salvation in you, to work out God's will in you? What does it look like to abide in Christ?

### WE *WILL BE* SAVED

5. Do you have a hard time trusting God's promises regarding caring for you, being sufficient for you, and securing your future? Who or what do you rely on to secure your future?

**6.** Write down some of the things you love. Have any of those replaced God as the biggest desire or love in your life? How is God "of first importance" (a better goal for our love and purpose), over anything else you love?

---

FOR EXTRA STUDY

**7.** Whether you've been a Christian for decades, or are just exploring the faith, take some time to explain briefly, in your own words what the gospel is. Once you finish, look back: does your explanation include past, present, and future elements of God's work and promise?

**8.** Based on your understanding of the gospel, in what areas of life do you need to "trade up" from a "lesser story, identity, hope, or savior" to see life through the better story of God? Or if you're not a follower of Jesus, consider that if God does all this in someone's life, why should they be inspired to "trade up"?

**9.** This week we've been focusing on knowing and believing we are forgiven and loved, we can do all things through Christ who gives us strength, and we have nothing to fear because God has our future in his hands. If you have kids, what are some ways you can model and teach this understanding of the gospel in your everyday life?

# PRAY

## WEEK 1, DAY 4

*Knowing that we're dependent on God to produce any good fruit in us, spend today walking through the following prayer exercises related to this week's theme.*

### PRAYING THE PSALMS

The Psalms teach us how to approach God in raw, humble ways, and help us remember the truth of who God objectively is, despite our subjective discomfort or circumstances. Slowly consider the words of the psalm, trying to understand it, lingering over it. Then pray it several times, as it is written or in your own words as a prayer to God.

**PSALM 63** *A Psalm of David, when he was in the wilderness of Judah.*

O God, you are my God; earnestly I seek you;
 my soul thirsts for you;
my flesh faints for you,
 as in a dry and weary land where there is no water.
So I have looked upon you in the sanctuary,
 beholding your power and glory.
Because your steadfast love is better than life,
 my lips will praise you.
So I will bless you as long as I live;
 in your name I will lift up my hands.
My soul will be satisfied as with fat and rich food,
 and my mouth will praise you with joyful lips,
when I remember you upon my bed,
 and meditate on you in the watches of the night;
for you have been my help,
 and in the shadow of your wings I will sing for joy.
My soul clings to you;
 your right hand upholds me.
But those who seek to destroy my life
 shall go down into the depths of the earth;
they shall be given over to the power of the sword;
 they shall be a portion for jackals.
But the king shall rejoice in God;
 all who swear by him shall exult,
 for the mouths of liars will be stopped.

**PSALM 42** *To the choirmaster. A Maskil of the Sons of Korah.*

As a deer pants for flowing streams,
so pants my soul for you, O God.
My soul thirsts for God,
for the living God.
When shall I come and appear before God?
My tears have been my food
day and night,
while they say to me all the day long,
"Where is your God?"
These things I remember,
as I pour out my soul:
how I would go with the throng
and lead them in procession to the house of God
with glad shouts and songs of praise,
a multitude keeping festival.
Why are you cast down, O my soul,
and why are you in turmoil within me?
Hope in God; for I shall again praise him,
my salvation and my God.
My soul is cast down within me;
therefore I remember you
from the land of Jordan and of Hermon,
from Mount Mizar.
Deep calls to deep
at the roar of your waterfalls;
all your breakers and your waves
have gone over me.
By day the LORD commands his steadfast love,
and at night his song is with me,
a prayer to the God of my life.
I say to God, my rock:
"Why have you forgotten me?
Why do I go mourning
because of the oppression of the enemy?"
As with a deadly wound in my bones,
my adversaries taunt me,
while they say to me all the day long,
"Where is your God?"
Why are you cast down, O my soul,
and why are you in turmoil within me?
Hope in God; for I shall again praise him,
my salvation and my God.

## CRAFT YOUR OWN PRAYER

In your own words, spend some intentional time talking to and listening for God along this week's theme. We encourage you to write your prayer, as well as any thoughts that come to mind that God might be prompting. Test those thoughts against the truth of Scripture, as well as your community. Here are some things you might pray:

- Thank God for his past salvation: consider your life before he redeemed you and how he carried out that redemption. Praise him for his glorious work.
- Thank God for his ongoing salvation: consider areas of sin, immaturity, weakness, or faithlessness he's currently working on, and consider the things he's currently showing and teaching you. Praise him for any area of growth you're seeing, no matter how small.
- Thank God for his future salvation: consider the promises he's made for you, your provision, and your care—both in this life and in eternity. Praise him for your ability to rest in him, as the only true hope for tomorrow.
- Look back at your answers to yesterday's questions. As you do, consider what jumps out to you and ask God to reveal areas he's working on that you haven't noticed, where he wants to grow you and mature you as he makes you more holy.
- Repent for areas that you've tried to be your own redeemer or have forgotten his promises or have moved away from his salvation, power, and ability.
- Stop to listen, be still and quiet before God, and write down any thoughts that come to mind.

## HISTORIC PRAYER

In closing today's prayer exercises, ponder and pray the prayer below, which is pulled from historic Christian literature, and has been prayed by Jesus's disciples for many, many years.

CREATOR AND REDEEMER GOD,
Author of all existence, source of all blessedness,
I adore thee for making me capable of knowing thee,
for giving me reason and conscience,
for leading me to desire thee;
I praise thee for the revelation of thyself in the gospel,
for thy heart as a dwelling place of pity,
for thy thoughts of peace towards me,
for thy patience and thy graciousness,
for the vastness of thy mercy.
Thou hast moved my conscience to know how
the guilty can be pardoned,
the unholy sanctified,
the poor enriched.
May I be always amongst those who not only hear but know thee,
who walk with and rejoice in thee,
who take thee at thy word and find life there.
Keep me always longing
for a present salvation in Holy Spirit comforts and rejoicings,
for spiritual graces and blessings,
for help to value my duties as well as my privileges.
May I cherish simplicity and godly sincerity of character.
Help me to be in reality before thee
as in appearance I am before men,
to be religious before I profess religion,
to leave the world before I enter the church,
to set my affections on things above,
to shun forbidden follies and vanities,
to be a dispenser as well as a partaker of grace,
to be prepared to bear evil as well as to do good.
O God, make me worthy of this calling,
that the name of Jesus may be glorified in me and I in him.

VALLEY OF VISION, P.12

WEEK 1, DAY 5

*Take some time today, by yourself or with others in your faith community, to carry out the following exercises, as you wrap your life around this week's truth.*

Objectively, if you always believed that Jesus was better, you'd have no problem living God's greater story, loving God's people, and prioritizing God's mission. But every day, sin, idols, excuses, and pursuits for "lesser" stories get in the way: we disbelieve the gospel and God's promises.

1. Consider the following idols, which either keep the gospel from being central to your life, or which keep you from living as if it is. Each has a couple example phrases that might help define it—but those are only examples; there are other thoughts/words that display the idol as well! After you prayerfully read through the list a few times, star some of the idols you wrestle with, serve, or worship most.

| | | |
|---|---|---|
| **APPROVAL**<br>*I need to please God/others/myself* | **CONTROL**<br>*I need to run this*<br>*No one else can do this* | **INSECURITY**<br>*I don't want people to know ____*<br>*I'm not good enough for ____* |
| **REPUTATION**<br>*I need to be important/good in others' eyes* | **SUCCESS**<br>*I need to win/be the best/accomplish ____* | **LOGIC**<br>*This makes sense*<br>*It's what culture says is 'right'* |
| **SECURITY**<br>*I value my safety*<br>*This makes me uncomfortable* | **PLEASURE**<br>*This feels good/makes me happy*<br>*I like ____* | **KNOWLEDGE**<br>*I need to learn more/see every detail/ think well about ____* |
| **SUPERIORITY**<br>*I have to show you I'm the best/know the most* | **RECOGNITION**<br>*You need to know how good I am* | **ENTITLEMENT**<br>*I deserve this*<br>*I've earned this* |
| **BUSYNESS**<br>*I need my schedule to be full/to be needed* | **CONSUMERISM**<br>*I want ____/take but don't give/want what works for me* | **ALOOFNESS**<br>*I'll stay removed/won't commit/won't open up/won't submit* |
| **SELFISHNESS**<br>*I do what I want, when I want*<br>*I am #1* | **INDEPENDENCE**<br>*I'll do it myself / I don't need you*<br>*Don't tell me what to do* | ??? |

**2.** Once you complete the preceding exercise...

- In the first column below, write some of the idols you starred.
- In the second column, write some false truths that the idol causes you to believe.
- And in the final column, write ways that the idols and false truths keep you living a "lesser" story than Jesus's, and keeps you from living out the gospel in everyday life.

| IDOL I STARRED | GOD'S PROMISE(S) REJECTED | IMPACT ON MY LIFE |
|---|---|---|
| *I'm entitled* | *I think I deserve more than I have;*<br>*I think I have to earn things* | *I'm disappointed in others when I don't get things; I'm focused on myself;*<br>*I don't think of others* |
| | | |
| | | |
| | | |
| | | |
| | | |

**3.** In considering how to live as disciples of Jesus in the everyday stuff of life, prayerfully carry out the following exercise, using the scenarios below.

- In the first column, list one of the scenarios that resonates with you.
- In the second column, think about what aspects of God's gospel story are displayed by each scenario—how does each display your belief that Jesus is better?
- In the third column, consider which of the idols from above might keep you from carrying out each behavior.
- In the last column, write ways that Jesus has proved himself to be better than those idols.

Over-tipping (think 30+%) even if the service is horrible

Becoming a "regular" at a local restaurant or watering hole

Turning off your phone, disconnecting, and "Sabbathing" for a day

Moving into your mission field, even if cost of living is higher than commuting

Throwing a party for the poor, who can't repay you, instead of your friends (Luke 14:12-14)

Accepting the invitation of a non-believing friend to go to a party or happy hour, knowing fully that biblical principles will likely not be in full effect

Having an "open-door policy" with your community and neighbors at many meals throughout the week

Buying and serving good wine or beer at a cookout, even if you don't drink

Enrolling your child in the neighborhood school, instead of the better private school across town

Lovingly calling out sin in the life of someone in your community

Speaking the gospel into a non-believing co-worker's life and need

Living in such a way that your neighbors can actually see a difference in you – to the point they think you're kind of weird

Write a final scenario here that is a common struggle for you, and address it

| SCENARIO | HOW THIS DISPLAYS THE GOSPEL |
| --- | --- |
| *Over-tipping with bad service* | *God is generous; God blesses me even though I don't earn anything* |
| | |
| | |
| | |
| | |

| IDOLS THAT PROHIBIT THIS | HOW JESUS IS BETTER THAN THE IDOL |
| --- | --- |
| *Selfishness; entitlement; hope in money; need to earn things* | *He provides for me; gives me all I need; doesn't make me earn his blessing* |
| | |
| | |
| | |
| | |

WEEK 1, DAY 6

Start by having someone share their story. The goal in sharing stories is to listen for things to celebrate and thank God for, and to listen for themes or areas of life to ask questions about and speak truth in love, as you point each other toward Jesus. After they share, pray for the person who shared and ask who will share next week.

*Based on this week's reading, questions, prayers, and activities, honestly discuss questions like the following with your faith community. The tendency is going to want to stay general: get gritty and specific. Commit to putting your belief into action, by planning one or two specific ways to carry out each. Lovingly speak truth into areas of weakness, and figure out together how to encourage each other to infuse the gospel into this week's regular rhythms. And remember, some of this—maybe most of this—can't be limited to the one "official" meeting of your community each week, and this discussion is simply acknowledging who you are personally, as a redeemed follower of Jesus, as you do life together.*

1. From this week's personal preparation, what stood out to you? What was new? What was exciting/hopeful?

2. From this week's personal preparation, is there anything you're confused by/have questions about? What was difficult to read/ponder?

3. Take some time to celebrate areas that God has helped members of your community remember, have faith in, and live out the past, present, and future elements of Jesus's better story.

4. From the verses and prayer time this week, what are some truths, promises, and blessings God

revealed to you about Jesus, and his work in your life, that you'd forgotten or hadn't lived out? Thank God for his revelation.

5. What themes did you start to notice about your belief or disbelief in Jesus and what he's done, about sin/idols in your life that keep you from believing, about false hopes and false identities, etc.? How has God worked this week to help redeem some areas of disbelief, idolatry, etc.?

6. Was there anything that you came across this week that frustrated you, or that was difficult to accept or write, that you need to confess to or discuss with your community? If so, do that now or grab someone privately later in the week. Don't keep it hidden!

7. What are ways that you need each other, to help you battle the idols that keep you from living as if Jesus is better, and to remind you of his promises and better story?

8. Is there anything we've discussed tonight that anyone wants to commit to follow-up on or do together in the coming week or beyond? Why or why not?

# REST

## WEEK 1, DAY 7

Knowing we're all busy, and that we all get behind, one day each week doesn't have specific assignments. It's simply a "floating day off" to encourage you to rest and dwell on this week's theme. This day to rest and recreate is designed to break up your week, and to remind you of God's truth and promises: He is sufficient for our every need, we rely on His power and leading to accomplish anything good, we don't have to work to earn his approval, and He is in control regardless of our action or inaction.

WEEK 2

# Discipleship

# START

## WEEK 2, DAY 1

*Prayerfully and thoughtfully read this week's reading (or read chapters 7-10 of Saturate). As you read, circle, underline, write in the margins, and interact with concepts or ideas that are new, difficult, inspiring, etc.*

For video and additional resources pertaining to Week 2, visit:

www.saturatetheworld.com/fg/week2

The person and work of Jesus cannot remain as a mere mental construct, separate from the rest of life. The gospel changes us. It gives us new identities, goals, and pursuits. Jesus's past, present, and future work redefine how we think, live, work, and act. Because of the gospel, we are disciples of Jesus. By the power of God, the life of a Christian is a life of learning from Jesus, following him, and "growing up in every way into him" (Eph 4:15). In other words, the life of a follower of Jesus is a life of obeying Jesus.

### A NEW PERSPECTIVE

When he called the first of his disciples, he said, "Follow me, and I will make you fishers of men" (Matt. 4:19). They had been fishermen, but Jesus was calling them to fish for people. They responded by leaving everything—their families, their careers, their futures—to follow Jesus. It started in a boat and went out to the world. Those first disciples radically recentered everything in their lives around Jesus, his teaching, and his mission. Their lives became all about Jesus! He was that important to them.

Then, after he had trained them for more than three years, suffered and died for their sins, and risen from the grave, Jesus told them to meet him on a mountain before he ascended to heaven. On that mountain, he was going to give his final commission to them to make disciples of all people groups. Just as Jesus had called them to follow him, be changed by him, and obey him, he sent them out to call others to follow him as well. He was going to send them to the ends of the earth so that Jesus saturation might happen.

So they met Jesus on the mountain and worshiped him there, but some still doubted (Matt. 28:16-17). They were in, but not all in. Slow down and don't miss this: Jesus's disciples had seen everything they needed to see. Jesus had taught them all he needed to teach them. And they had experienced all they needed to experience with Jesus! And yet, some were still doubting. This is good news for me! Though I've walked with Jesus for more than twenty-four years, I still struggle with doubts. Maybe you do as well.

We're not alone! The disciples were still in process—a process that would last their lifetimes. And the same is true of us. That is what discipleship is all about. It is the ongoing process of submitting all of life to Jesus, and seeing him saturate your entire life and world with his presence and power. It's a process of daily growing in your awareness of your need for him in the everyday stuff of life. It is walking with Jesus, being filled with Jesus, and being led by Jesus in every place and in every way.

Read the previous paragraph again—we hope it's a helpful definition of discipleship!

## PAYING IT FORWARD

Once we start to realize that discipleship is an everyday, all-of-life process for our own lives, we're halfway to understanding God's call. The other half of that call is seen most clearly in the great commission, where God calls his people—*all his people*—to "make disciples of all nations, baptizing them in the name of the Father and of the Son and of the Holy Spirit, teaching them to observe all that I have commanded you" (Matt. 28:19-20). Part of our own discipleship is "paying it forward": seeing God not only work *in* us, for our own discipleship, but also seeing him work *through* us, for others' discipleship. In fact, the Apostle Paul tells us that a primary way we grow into maturity in Christ is through "speaking the truth in love" to and with each other (Eph 4:15-16). God didn't design discipleship to primarily happen alone.

All-of-life discipleship—learning to follow, trust, and obey Jesus in the everyday stuff of life, and training others to do the same—requires submitting to and obeying God's Word in three key environments: life on life, life in community, and life on mission.

## LIFE ON LIFE

God's means of [your growth, redemption, and] restoration is others in your life who are committed to bringing your brokenness out into the open and bringing the gospel of Jesus to bear on it. The layers with which we've covered ourselves have to be pulled back, and we can't do that kind of work alone. We have to get close. We have to be seen and known. This is what we call life-on-life discipleship—life that is lived up close so that we are visible and accessible to one another, so that others can gently peel back the layers and join us in our restoration.

Jesus lived life with his disciples. He was close enough to really know them. He observed what they believed by watching how they lived. He became closely acquainted with their brokenness so that he could see their wrong thinking, wrong believing, and wrong acting. They were exposed. And as they were exposed, Jesus helped them to be restored.

## LIFE IN COMMUNITY

If you look at the life and ministry of Jesus, and subsequently the ministry of the apostle Paul, you certainly would not come to the conclusion that one-on-one discipleship is best. Jesus discipled his followers while they experienced life together in community. We know they "got it" because the story of how they continued to live tells us they were devoted to one another in the day-to-day stuff of everyday life. Jesus's way of discipleship cannot happen in one-on-one meetings alone.

The church is Jesus's body. It has many parts, but it is one body, so it takes many of us committed to each other's development to help us each become more like Jesus. We all need many people who love Jesus around us to do this. Every person in Christ's body is meant to work this way. You are meant to play a part in equipping and encouraging others. God intends for all of us to actively engage in disciple-making in light of our unique design so that we both do the work and equip others to do it.

## LIFE ON MISSION

Jesus didn't say, "Show up to class and I will train you." Nor did he say, "Attend synagogue and that will be sufficient." No, he called the disciples to join him on the mission ("Follow me"), and while they were on the mission with him, he trained them to be disciple-makers ("I will make you fishers of men").

In other words, Jesus taught them the basics of making disciples while they were on the mission of making disciples. They could observe everything Jesus said and did. They could see how he rebuked the religious leaders who tried to make it harder for people to come to God. They were able to watch his compassion and care of people being ruined by sin. They couldn't overlook his willingness to heal and help the broken. And the power he exerted over demons was clearly on display. They listened, watched, and learned in the everyday stuff of life. After a while, he invited them to share in some of the work he was doing. Sure, they messed up, a lot, but he was there to help, to correct, to clean up—to train them—while they were on his mission. They were in a disciple-making residency with Jesus.

After the disciples had spent time watching, learning, and practicing under Jesus's watchful eye, he sent them out to begin to practice what he had taught them. He did not send them out alone; they went together. Then they returned and reported to Jesus what they had experienced. All did not go perfectly. So he trained them in the areas of their weaknesses and failures. He did this kind of ongoing training with them for more than three years. As a result, when he finally ascended to heaven, they had been prepared to fulfill the mission. The best training for mission happens while on mission.

## MISSIONAL COMMUNITIES

The necessity of these three environments is the basis for what are commonly called "missional communities." The Christian life—and the gospel identities and rhythms we'll start to consider next week—cannot be lived alone, nor can it be carried out as one person among several dozen or a few thousand, which is the context of many American church gatherings. Instead, the best venue for living as disciples of Jesus happens in the context of a few other disciples, mutually committed to growing each other's lives and faith, pursuing God's mission together.

Missional communities are not programs of a church; missional communities *are* the Church. In other words, the way God intends his people to live and thrive as disciples of Jesus is in the context of a community, growing in the gospel and on mission together. It's in this type of community that life on life, life in community, and life on mission discipleship most easily happen.

---

## DAY 1: QUESTIONS TO CONSIDER

1. Circle the discipleship environment most familiar to you. In the space below, explain why. Put a box around the environment in which you're least comfortable? Why?

   *Life on life* *Life in community* *Life on mission*

**2.** What experience have you had "speaking the truth in love" with other followers of Jesus?

**3.** Are you currently on mission with others, together discovering your need for God's power and grace? If so, who are those you're on mission with? If not, are there areas of your life where growth/discipleship are lacking, which would be well served by such a group?

# READ

## WEEK 2, DAY 2

*Prayerfully and thoughtfully read the biblical texts below, then spend a few moments reflecting on the truths therein by answering the questions at the end.*

Where do you see this week's three environments in the following verses, whether explicitly mentioned, implied by actions, or as simply necessary to rightly understand the passage?

◘ Box areas you see life-on-life discipleship

○ Circle areas you see discipleship happening in community

★ Star areas you see discipleship happening on a common mission

### LUKE 10:1-11, 17

After this the Lord appointed seventy-two others and sent them on ahead of him, two by two, into every town and place where he himself was about to go. And he said to them, "The harvest is plentiful, but the laborers are few. Therefore pray earnestly to the Lord of the harvest to send out laborers into his harvest. Go your way; behold, I am sending you out as lambs in the midst of wolves. Carry no moneybag, no knapsack, no sandals, and greet no one on the road. Whatever house you enter, first say, 'Peace be to this house!' And if a son of peace is there, your peace will rest upon him. But if not, it will return to you. And remain in the same house, eating and drinking what they provide, for the laborer deserves his wages. Do not go from house to house. Whenever you enter a town and they receive you, eat what is set before you. Heal the sick in it and say to them, 'The kingdom of God has come near to you.' But whenever you enter a town and they do not receive you, go into its streets and say, 'Even the dust of your town that clings to our feet we wipe off against you. Nevertheless know this, that the kingdom of God has come near'... The seventy-two returned with joy, saying, "Lord, even the demons are subject to us in your name!"

### ACTS 2:42-47

And they devoted themselves to the apostles' teaching and the fellowship, to the breaking of bread and the prayers. And awe came upon every soul, and many wonders and signs were being done through the apostles. And all who believed were together and had all things in common. And they were selling their possessions and belongings and distributing the proceeds to all, as any had need. And day by day, attending the temple together and breaking bread in their homes, they received their food with glad and generous hearts, praising God and having favor with all the people. And the Lord added to their number day by day those who were being saved.

### ROMANS 12:4-8

For as in one body we have many members, and the members do not all have the same function, so we, though many, are one body in Christ, and individually members one of another. Having gifts that differ according to the grace given to us, let us use them: if prophecy, in proportion to our faith; if service, in our serving; the one who teaches, in his teaching; the one who exhorts, in his exhortation; the one who contributes, in generosity; the one who leads, with zeal; the one who does acts of mercy, with cheerfulness.

### 1 CORINTHIANS 12: 12-26

For just as the body is one and has many members, and all the members of the body, though many, are one body, so it is with Christ. For in one Spirit we were all baptized into one body—Jews or Greeks, slaves or free—and all were made to drink of one Spirit.

For the body does not consist of one member but of many. If the foot should say, "Because I am not a hand, I do not belong to the body," that would not make it any less a part of the body. And if the ear should say, "Because I am not an eye, I do not belong to the body," that would not make it any less a part of the body. If the whole body were an eye, where would be the sense of hearing? If the whole body were an ear, where would be the sense of smell? But as it is, God arranged the members in the body, each one of them, as he chose. If all were a single member, where would the body be? As it is, there are many parts, yet one body.

The eye cannot say to the hand, "I have no need of you," nor again the head to the feet, "I have no need of you." On the contrary, the parts of the body that seem to be weaker are indispensable, and on those parts of the body that we think less honorable we bestow the greater honor, and our unpresentable parts are treated with greater modesty, which our more presentable parts do not require. But God has so composed the body, giving greater honor to the part that lacked it, that there may be no division in the body, but that the members may have the same care for one another. If one member suffers, all suffer together; if one member is honored, all rejoice together.

### EPHESIANS 4:11-16

And he gave the apostles, the prophets, the evangelists, the shepherds and teachers, to equip the saints for the work of ministry, for building up the body of Christ, until we all attain to the unity of the faith and of the knowledge of the Son of God, to mature manhood, to the measure of the stature of the fullness of Christ, so that we may no longer be children, tossed to and fro by the waves and carried about by every wind of doctrine, by human cunning, by craftiness in deceitful schemes. Rather, speaking the truth in love, we are to grow up in every way into him who is the head, into Christ, from whom the whole body, joined and held together by every joint with which it is equipped, when each part is working properly, makes the body grow so that it builds itself up in love.

### HEBREWS 5:12-14

For though by this time you ought to be teachers, you need someone to teach you again the basic principles of the oracles of God. You need milk, not solid food, for everyone who lives on milk is unskilled in the word of righteousness, since he is a child. But solid food is for the mature, for those who have their powers of discernment trained by constant practice to distinguish good from evil.

---

## DAY 2: QUESTIONS TO CONSIDER

Answer these questions as you contemplate what you saw in today's verses:

**1.** What themes jumped out to you as you considered these texts?

**2.** Look back through these verses: what are some of the areas of life that were "discipled"? What was the venue in which this discipleship took place?

**3.** How do these verses inform the biblical teaching that every follower of Jesus is "a disciple, sent to make disciples who make disciples?"

**4.** Are Jesus's and Paul's examples of involving disciples in the hands-on work of ministry while they're still in training—indeed, as part of their training—different than what you've experienced?

What thoughts or questions does this raise in you?

There are plenty of stories, verses, and instances in the Bible where God's people didn't rest in the truths of the gospel. Think about what you know of the Bible and Story of God and answer the following questions. If you need a jumpstart, consider these passages: Exodus 32; Judges 2:11-15; 1 Kings 11; Acts 12:20-25; 1 Corinthians 3:1-9.

**5.** What are other things that people became disciples of in the Bible—things other than God that they obeyed, followed, and pursued?

**6.** As you consider those situations, what was it that led each person/group to become a disciple of something other than Jesus? Are there ways that this week's discipleship environments could have helped?

# THINK

## WEEK 2, DAY 3

*Knowing that each week builds on previous weeks, prayerfully and honestly work through these questions and exercises, in light of previous weeks' and this week's themes.*

Often "Christian maturity" is spoken of as an objective, across-the-board measurement. People say, "She's mature" or "He's a new believer" in the same way they say, "She's a woman," or "He's middle-aged." But one of the themes in the Bible is that every follower of Jesus is gifted in different areas of life and faith; another theme is that we must "grow up *in every way* into Christ who is the head" (Eph. 4:15; emphasis added).

If this latter view is true, then instead of one's maturity being defined as one objective standard, the truth is that every follower of Jesus—no matter how long ago they were redeemed—has areas of strength and areas they need help. I may be generous, but lacking in humility; I may have a friend who knows many Bible verses, but is weak in sharing the gospel. And so it goes, for every disciple of Jesus. This is why all-of-life discipleship is so important: God gave us different gifts—"for the building up of the body" (Eph. 4:12; 1 Cor. 12:12-26; Rom. 12:4-8)—and why the way to grow up is "speaking the truth in love" (Eph. 4:15). We need each other, to grow up together into Christ!

---

### DAY 3: QUESTIONS TO CONSIDER

Consider how these truths play out in your mind and life, by asking yourself the following questions in light of this week's theme. Don't feel like you need to answer every question: instead, choose those that most resonate with you, that you feel God the Spirit speaking to you through, or maybe those that are most challenging to you—either way, we encourage you to answer at least one question from each section, and to write down your answers.

#### LIFE ON LIFE

1. Who knows you well enough to peel back layers and speak the truth of the gospel into areas of need or disbelief?

2. In chapter 8 of *Saturate*, Jeff writes, "We have found that conflict pushes what is already in the heart to the surface. Therefore, it often serves to remove the façade." How does life on life discipleship help remove façades and display what's truly in someone's heart?

LIFE IN COMMUNITY

3. Considering today's opening paragraph, write some areas of your life and faith you're gifted or "mature," by the grace of God, as well as areas of your life and faith you're weak or "immature."

How would that impact someone if they were "being discipled" by you alone?

4. Who in your community or neighborhood is strong in areas you're weak, and how might you ask them to help you grow? At the same time, who is weak in areas God has made you strong, and how might you offer to serve them?

### LIFE ON MISSION

**5.** What experience have you had "learning on mission" from others—being trained for God's mission while living on God's mission? How was that training beneficial? In what ways was it hard?

**6.** If "life on mission is not just about being disciples, but also about *making* disciples who make disciples," why can that only be learned while on Jesus's mission?

---

### FOR EXTRA STUDY

**7.** Do you have a community of people with whom you pursue growth in life and faith? How do your gifts and areas of maturity serve each other? In what ways can you pursue each other better?

**8.** While some aspects of discipleship happen at formal events (such as Sunday gatherings, group meetings, or one-on-one meetings), what are other venues for discipleship—times and place in your everyday life that you can spend time with others?

**9.** Why was it important for Jesus's disciples to actually see Jesus in action, before he ascended and left them to carry out his mission, make disciples, and lead the Church?

WEEK 2, DAY 4

*Knowing that we're dependent on God to produce any good fruit in us, spend today walking through the following prayer exercises related to this week's theme.*

## PRAYING THE PSALMS & PROVERBS

God's wisdom literature teaches us how to approach God in raw, humble ways, and help us remember the truth of who God objectively is, despite our subjective discomfort or circumstances. Slowly consider the words of the psalm and proverbs below, trying to understand it, lingering over it. Then pray it several times as it is written or in your own words as a prayer to God.

**PSALM 133** *A Song of Ascents. Of David.*

Behold, how good and pleasant it is
when brothers dwell in unity!
It is like the precious oil on the head,
running down on the beard,
on the beard of Aaron,
running down on the collar of his robes!
It is like the dew of Hermon,
which falls on the mountains of Zion!
For there the LORD has commanded the blessing,
life forevermore.

**PROVERBS 27:5-6, 17**

Better is open rebuke than hidden love.
Faithful are the wounds of a friend; profuse are the kisses of an enemy...
Iron sharpens iron, and one man sharpens another.

**PROVERBS 18:1-8**

Whoever isolates himself seeks his own desire; he breaks out against all sound judgment.
A fool takes no pleasure in understanding, but only in expressing his opinion.
When wickedness comes, contempt comes also, and with dishonor comes disgrace.
The words of a man's mouth are deep waters; the fountain of wisdom is a bubbling brook.
It is not good to be partial to the wicked or to deprive the righteous of justice.
A fool's lips walk into a fight, and his mouth invites a beating.
A fool's mouth is his ruin, and his lips are a snare to his soul.
The words of a whisperer are like delicious morsels; they go down into the inner parts of the body.

## CRAFT YOUR OWN PRAYER

In your own words, spend some intentional time talking to and listening for God along this week's theme. We encourage you to write your prayer, as well as thoughts that come to mind that God might be prompting. Test those thoughts against the truth of Scripture, as well as your community. Here are some things you might pray:

- Praise God for giving you others with whom to walk this Christian life, to speak into your growth, and to share your mission of being a disciple who makes disciples.

- If—whether intentionally or otherwise—you've ignored the corporate reality of following Jesus or have been too prideful to admit your need for others or have even withheld your gifts from other followers of Jesus who need those gifts, ask God to reveal your motives, then confess and repent to him, asking him to help redeem individualistic views of discipleship.

- Thank God for the areas of life and faith he's made you strong, and ask him to reveal to you ways that those gifts can be used to serve those God has put in your life—whether followers of Jesus or not.

- If you're not in a community on mission, ask God to bring people to mind who might join you in coming together to live out this all-of-life discipleship, and to make disciples together.

- Look back at your answers to yesterday's questions. As you do, consider what jumps out to you, and ask God to reveal anything you haven't considered before regarding his design for discipleship, life on life, in community, and on mission.

- Stop to listen, be still and quiet before God, and write down any thoughts that come to mind.

## HISTORIC PRAYER

In closing today's prayer exercises, ponder and pray the prayer below, which is pulled from historic Christian literature, and has been prayed by Jesus's disciples for many, many years.

> Lord Jesus, let me know myself and know You, and desire nothing save only You.
> Let me hate myself and love You.
> Let me do everything for the sake of You.
> Let me humble myself and exalt You.
> Let me think of nothing except You.
> Let me die to myself and live in You.
> Let me accept whatever happens as from You.
> Let me banish self and follow You, and ever desire to follow You.
> Let me fly from myself and take refuge in You,
> That I may deserve to be defended by You.
> Let me fear for myself.
> Let me fear You, and let me be among those who are chosen by You.
> Let me distrust myself and put my trust in You.
> Let me be willing to obey for the sake of You.
> Let me cling to nothing save only to You,
> And let me be poor because of You.
> Look upon me, that I may love You.
> Call me that I may see You, and for ever enjoy You. Amen.

**ST. AUGUSTINE OF HIPPO, 354 – 430 AD**

## WEEK 2, DAY 5

*Take some time today, by yourself or with others in your faith community, to carry out the following exercises, as you wrap your life around this week's truth.*

Today's three activities are designed to help you move toward elements of life on life discipleship, as well as discipleship in community and discipleship on mission.

**1.** Life on life discipleship:

- In the first column on the next page, write areas of life that those in your community have helped you grow that aren't overtly "Christian" things (For example: instead of things like Bible study, prayer, or accountability, think of ways they've helped you grow in things such as learning to have conflict well with your spouse or roommates, disciplining children, money or anger management, learning a life skill.)
- In the second column, write the name(s) of those who carried out the help, and the setting it happened (For example: "dinner table," "morning commute.")
- In the final column, consider how each of those "everyday life" areas actually relates to biblical principles, reflects the gospel, and is it a means of following Jesus—in other words, how is each an element of life on life discipleship?

| AREA OF GROWTH | NAME & SETTING | REFLECTION OF DISCIPLESHIP |
|---|---|---|
| *Withholding discipline when I'm angry* | *Alison W; living room, after the toy broke* | *Discipline > punishment (correction > penance); God withholds wrath from me but corrects my errors* |
| | | |
| | | |
| | | |
| | | |

**2.** Discipleship in community:

- In the space below, consider the specific gifts and areas of maturity of others in your community. Think of specific ways God has used different people to bless, encourage, serve, and grow you—no matter how small or practical, and *especially* people you don't naturally "get."
- Pause and thank God for that person and the ways they've helped you grow; ask him to help you know how to serve them, and if necessary, to soften your heart toward them and the ways you're different.
- Actually write a note, email, or text to each person, celebrating God's gifting and thanking them for those specific ways they've served your discipleship.

| COMMUNITY MEMBER | HOW THEY'VE BLESSED ME |
|---|---|
| *Justin T.* | *Helps me see the blessing of creating margin and slowing down; helps me understand introspection & taking time to "look back"* |
| | |
| | |
| | |
| | |
| | |

**3.** Discipleship on mission:

- In the first column below, write down some of the things you do in your weekly or monthly rhythm of life—whether Christian disciplines, areas you engage for service or mission, hobbies/recreation, family life, chores, etc.
- In the second column below, write the name(s) of people in your community you could start to share those things with, and some of the areas of life and faith you'd like to discuss/practice with them, as a means of discipleship on mission.
- Call at least one of those people and ask them to meet up for that activity within the next week or so.

| THINGS I REGULARLY DO | PEOPLE WHO COULD JOIN ME AND HOW |
|---|---|
| *Work out at school gym* | *Davinion – since I'm a freshman, he could help me meet people in our fraternity working out there* |
| | |
| | |
| | |
| | |
| | |

WEEK 2, DAY 6

Start by having someone share their story. The goal in sharing stories is to listen for things to celebrate and thank God for, and to listen for themes or areas of life to ask questions and speak truth in love, as you point each other toward Jesus. After they share, pray for the person who shared and ask who will share next week.

*Based on this week's reading, questions, prayers, and activities, honestly discuss questions like the following with your faith community. The tendency is going to want to stay general: get gritty and specific. Commit to putting your belief into action, by planning one or two specific ways to carry out each. Lovingly speak truth into areas of weakness, and figure out together how to encourage each other to infuse the gospel into this week's regular rhythms. And remember, some of this – maybe most of this – can't be limited to the one "official" meeting of your community each week, and this discussion is simply acknowledging who you are personally, as a redeemed follower of Jesus, as you do life together.*

**1.** From this week's personal preparation, what stood out to you? What was new? What was exciting/hopeful?

**2.** From this week's personal preparation, is there anything you're confused by/have questions about? What was difficult to read/ponder?

**3.** Since one of this week's big themes was our need of each other's strengths in our own areas of growth, share some of the ways that others have discipled you in everyday life, in community, and/or on mission that you wrote down on Days 3 and 5.

**4.** Ephesians 4:11 talks about five "people gifts" God gives to the body. Jesus fulfills all five of these roles fully and completely. [But] if we are to grow up into the fullness of our head, Jesus, we need every one of these people gifts providing an example for us, while also encouraging and equipping us ... When each of these people gifts does what he or she is uniquely designed by God to do, they equip the others to grow up in that ability as well (vv. 12-16). As we consider these types of community, which is each person's most natural gift or two? And how do the rest of us need their help to grow in our own areas of weakness? If we don't know someone's primary giftings, why? How can we know them better, or help them understand their gifting?

**Apostles**/missionaries move outward toward those who don't yet have faith in Jesus, and they encourage others in the body to be outward-moving missionaries as well, both by example and through encouragement and equipping.

**Prophets** have the ability to speak very direct and timely words that encourage or exhort people to remember what God has said and to move forward toward what God wants.

**Evangelists** winsomely draw people toward Jesus and his body, and help others grow in sharing the gospel.

**Shepherds** are particularly designed to ensure people are well cared for and, in turn, care for one another.

**Teachers** have the skill to methodically explain and equip people to know and obey God's Word.

**5.** What are ways we can ensure each other's growth in maturity, beyond simple knowledge about God and the Bible—in our meetings and throughout each week?

**6.** How well does our community do with each of these three environments: life on life, life in community, and life on mission? How can we serve each other and help promote all three of these more effectively?

**7.** How can we grow in our culture of pushing through façades and speaking truth in love to each other?

**8.** Is there anything we've discussed tonight that anyone wants to commit to follow-up on or do together in the coming week or beyond? Why or why not?

⊙ *Close your meeting in prayer.*

# REST

## WEEK 2, DAY 7

Knowing we're all busy, and that we all get behind, one day each week doesn't have specific assignments. It's simply a "floating day off" to encourage you to rest and dwell on this week's theme. This day to rest and recreate is designed to break up your week, and to remind you of God's truth and promises: He is sufficient for our every need, we rely on His power and leading to accomplish anything good, we don't have to work to earn his approval, and He is in control regardless of our action or inaction.

WEEK 3

NEW IDENTITY

# Family

# START

## WEEK 3, DAY 1

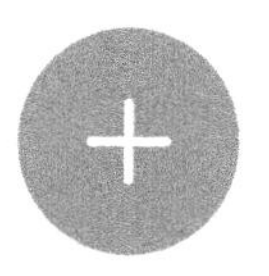

*Prayerfully and thoughtfully read this week's reading (or read chapters 11-12 of Saturate). As you read, circle, underline, write in the margins, and interact with concepts or ideas that are new, difficult, inspiring, etc.*

For video and additional resources pertaining to Week 3, visit:

www.saturatetheworld.com/fg/week3

Throughout the New Testament, whenever the people in the churches that Paul influenced went sideways, Paul didn't just confront their wrongdoing and tell them what to do. He started by reminding them of who God is, what he had done for them in Jesus, and who they were in light of that. Then, he reminded them of how believing the truth about the gospel and their new identity would lead them to a different behavior. Paul knew that all of our behaviors are the result of what we believe about who God is as revealed through what God does, leading to what we believe about who we are. God's work in Jesus Christ grants us a whole new identity, and this new identity leads to a whole new way of living.

We do what we do because of who we are. You do who you are. Being precedes doing. God is and God does. And he does who he is. His activity reveals the truth about who he is.

### CREATION: TRUE AND FALSE IDENTITIES

This week is the first of three in which we'll consider our gospel identities. Our identity informs everything we do, and our identity is founded on who God is and his work in us. We see this truth from the first pages of the Bible, in the story of God's perfect creation.

God is the Creator (who he is) who created (what he did) images of himself (who we are) to create and co-create (what we do). Do you see the progression? Who God is (Creator) is revealed through what God has done (created), which leads to who we are (image bearers created in God's likeness) and what we do (display God and co-create more image bearers).

Adam and Eve's perfect identity only lasted for about a page and half of our Bibles, at which point an evil Tempter enters God's garden and says, "Don't look to God to define you, to declare you good! Look elsewhere. Look to what I say will make you great. Look to yourself. Look to what you do!" Pause here for a moment: who or what is defining you? Are you letting someone or something other than God's Word and work define you? Are you defining yourself? Are you looking to your own abilities and actions to make you who you are? Are you looking to what has been done to you or what you hope will be done to you to define you?

## OUR NEW IDENTITIES, IN THE GOSPEL

All humanity falls into the Tempter's lie with shattered relationship with God and shattered identities. But thankfully, God was not content to leave his creation in this shattered condition.

After Jesus died and rose again, just before he ascended back to the right hand of the Father, he commissioned his disciples, saying: "All authority in heaven and on earth has been given to me. Go therefore and make disciples of all nations, baptizing them in the name of the Father and of the Son and of the Holy Spirit, teaching them to observe all that I have commanded you. And behold, I am with you always, to the end of the age" (Matt. 28:18-20).

Jesus had claimed back the authority that Adam and Eve had given away, and he was bringing about a new beginning—a new creation. This new creation has a new people—people who were dead in their sins and defined by the works of sinful humanity, but who are now alive in Christ and defined by Jesus, the better Word and the better work. Paul says to the church in Corinth: "Therefore, if anyone is in Christ, he is a new creation. The old has passed away; behold, the new has come" (2 Cor. 5:17).

This is why Jesus commands that we baptize disciples in the name of the Father, the Son, and the Holy Spirit. Our baptism is a physical display of our old life of sin and death being buried with Jesus Christ in his death. It is also a sign of our new life of faith, hope, and love, as we have been raised with Christ into new life. We have a new life, a new identity, and a new name. Just as Abram was given a new name that represented what God had done and would do through him, our new name represents what God has done and will do through us.

## WE ARE FAMILY: BAPTIZED INTO THE NAME OF THE FATHER

Because of who God is and what God has done in the gospel, our new identities are as family, servants, and missionaries. The identity we consider this week is that of "family."

If your life is now hidden with Christ Jesus (Col. 3:3), God dearly loves you, regardless of what you've done or will do. Just as God the Father loves the Son, so he loves you. Just as the Father said of Jesus the Son, "This is my beloved Son, with whom I am well pleased" (Matt. 3:17), he now says the same over you. You are a child of God, part of his family. This is your new identity, for you have been baptized in the name of the Father. As a result, you have a new name: Child of the Father. Son of God. Daughter of God. If you believe this to be true, it changes how you live and how you love. What God has done to you, he now wants to do through you.

Above, we briefly considered who God is and what he has done, as well as who we are and what we are to do. Let's think through those categories again in light of our baptism in the name of the Father. Consider these four questions: Who is God? He is our Father. What has he done? He has loved us by sending his Son, Jesus, to die for our sins. Who are we? We are the dearly loved children of God—God's family. If we believe this, what do we do? We love one another as brothers and sisters in the same way God has loved us.

## LIVING OUT OUR FAMILY IDENTITY WITH OTHER PEOPLE

God has perfectly loved you so that, through you, he might love others. He pours his perfect love into your heart through his Spirit in order that you might love others with the love he gives you. When you believe the gospel regarding God's love for you, you love others because he loved you first. If you believe God dearly loves you, you will love others in the same ways he loves you. You will love others like family.

Think about where you live. Do you know your neighbors? Has God given you a heart to love them like family? What would it look like if you did? What about the people in your small group or missional community? Do you love one another this way? How might your group change if you did?

Now think about who God has sent you to (your neighbors, coworkers, peers at school, and others). What might it look like if you were to love them as if they were your brothers and sisters? Like children of our Father in heaven? "But they're not," you might say. "They don't yet belong to God." Yes, but we don't know whom he is drawing to himself. And how will they ever come to know the love of God the Father if they don't experience it through us? Consider those God has put around you as the lost children of God who don't yet know how much their Father loves them. Then show them his Fatherly love in tangible ways.

## LIVING OUT OUR FAMILY IDENTITY THROUGH THE POWER OF GOD

We love because we were first loved. And we love with the same love with which he loved us. When we fail to love, we show we don't yet fully know the love of God for us. We don't know who God is, what he has done, and who we are in Christ.

We need the Spirit of God to continue to reveal these truths to our hearts, to pour the love of God the Father into our hearts that we might love others with the same love and in the same way he has loved us. Baptized into the name of the Father, we are his family so that we might love one another as he has loved us.

God has perfectly loved you so that, through you, he might love others. He pours his perfect love into your heart through his Spirit in order that you might love others with the love he gives you. When you believe the gospel regarding God's love for you, you love others because he loved you first. If you believe God dearly loves you, you will love others in the same ways he loves you. You will love others like family.

---

## DAY 1: QUESTIONS TO CONSIDER

1. What are some of the ways the Bible speaks of our relationship with God the Father, God the Son, and God the Spirit in familial terms?

2. What are some of the ways the Bible speaks of our relationships with other followers of Jesus—and other humans, made in the image of God—in familial terms?

3. Whether you've experienced this or not, what are some ways that healthy nuclear families love each other? How should our new identity in the gospel lead us to even greater love?

4. Do you have a hard time considering yourself a son or daughter of God, and a brother or sister of Jesus and others? Why? If you need help believing this, we encourage you to reach out to someone in your community and walk through your disbelief and need in this area.

# READ

## WEEK 3, DAY 2

*Prayerfully and thoughtfully read the biblical texts below, then spend a few moments reflecting on the truths therein by answering the questions at the end.*

Where do you see the Bible speak of the depth of our relationships, whether explicitly mentioned, implied by actions, or as simply necessary to rightly understand the passage?

- ◘ Box areas you see a familial relationship between God the Father, Son, and Spirit
- ○ Circle areas you see the familial relationship of God and his people
- ★ Star areas you see the familial relationship of God's people with each other

### JOHN 5:19-20

So Jesus said to them, "Truly, truly, I say to you, the Son can do nothing of his own accord, but only what he sees the Father doing. For whatever the Father does, that the Son does likewise. For the Father loves the Son and shows him all that he himself is doing. And greater works than these will he show him, so that you may marvel.

### ACTS 2:42-47

And they devoted themselves to the apostles' teaching and the fellowship, to the breaking of bread and the prayers. And awe came upon every soul, and many wonders and signs were being done through the apostles. And all who believed were together and had all things in common. And they were selling their possessions and belongings and distributing the proceeds to all, as any had need. And day by day, attending the temple together and breaking bread in their homes, they received their food with glad and generous hearts, praising God and having favor with all the people. And the Lord added to their number day by day those who were being saved.

### ROMANS 8:14-17

For all who are led by the Spirit of God are sons of God. For you did not receive the spirit of slavery to fall back into fear, but you have received the Spirit of adoption as sons, by whom we cry, "Abba! Father!" The Spirit himself bears witness with our spirit that we are children of God, and if children, then heirs—heirs of God and fellow heirs with Christ, provided we suffer with him in order that we may also be glorified with him.

**1 THESSALONIANS 2:7-12**

But we were gentle among you, like a nursing mother taking care of her own children. So, being affectionately desirous of you, we were ready to share with you not only the gospel of God but also our own selves, because you had become very dear to us. For you remember, brothers, our labor and toil: we worked night and day, that we might not be a burden to any of you, while we proclaimed to you the gospel of God. You are witnesses, and God also, how holy and righteous and blameless was our conduct toward you believers. For you know how, like a father with his children, we exhorted each one of you and encouraged you and charged you to walk in a manner worthy of God, who calls you into his own kingdom and glory.

**1 TIMOTHY 5:1-8**

Do not rebuke an older man but encourage him as you would a father, younger men as brothers, older women as mothers, younger women as sisters, in all purity. Honor widows who are truly widows. But if a widow has children or grandchildren, let them first learn to show godliness to their own household and to make some return to their parents, for this is pleasing in the sight of God. She who is truly a widow, left all alone, has set her hope on God and continues in supplications and prayers night and day, but she who is self-indulgent is dead even while she lives. Command these things as well, so that they may be without reproach. But if anyone does not provide for his relatives, and especially for members of his household, he has denied the faith and is worse than an unbeliever.

---

**FOR MORE:**

Isaiah 43:6-7 / Ezekiel 36:26-28 / John 1:12-13 / Ephesians 1:3-12 / 1 John 4:7-21 / Ephesians 4:15-16

## DAY 2: QUESTIONS TO CONSIDER

Answer these questions as you contemplate what you saw in today's verses:

1. What themes jumped out to you as you considered these texts?

2. Look back through these verses: what are some of the familial things that the biblical authors describe God's people doing, as they lived as a family?

3. The Acts passage starts by saying that Jesus's followers "devoted themselves" to God and each other: what does "devoted" mean? And in your mind, does it aptly describe your posture toward God, those in your community, and those in your mission field?

**4.** How does the tribal culture of Israel (God's Old Covenant people) further inform God's design for his people, that it's always been a corporate lifestyle of pursuing obedience and faith together? How does this inform our understanding of "Church"?

There are plenty of stories, verses, and instances in the Bible where God's people didn't rest in the truths of the gospel. Think about what you know of the Bible and Story of God and answer the following questions. If you need a jumpstart, consider these passages: Leviticus 13:38-46; Proverbs 11:13; Proverbs 18:1-2; Galatians 2:11-14; Hebrews 10:24-25.

**5.** Who are some of the people described throughout the Bible living outside of familial relationships with God and his people (Old Testament Israel, Jesus's band of disciples, the New Testament church, etc.)? How are they described?

**6.** Other than seasons of preparation, can you think of examples of God's people living in isolation in the Bible, rather than being open and vulnerable? If so, which of those were healthy and which weren't? Why do you think that is?

# THINK
## WEEK 3, DAY 3

*Knowing that each week builds on previous weeks, prayerfully and honestly work through these questions and exercises, in light of previous weeks' and this week's themes.*

Consider how our Family Identity plays out in your mind and life by asking yourself the following questions in light of this week's theme. Don't feel like you need to answer every question: instead, choose those that most resonate with you, that you feel God the Spirit speaking to you through, or maybe those that are most challenging to you—either way, we encourage you to answer at least one question from each section, and to write down your answers.

### DAY 3: QUESTIONS TO CONSIDER

**In addition to the answers given to these questions for Day 1's reading, consider these aspects of God's story, thinking specifically in familial terms:**

1. Who is God and what are some of the things He has done (in regards to himself, his creation, and his people)?
   *[In saying "his people" in these two questions, think of your personal experience, as well as those he's drawn into his family and those he hasn't yet, who are still created in the image of God for his glory.]*

2. Who are we and what do we do (in regards to God, his creation, and his people)?

**CONSIDER OUR FAMILIAL RELATIONSHIP WITH GOD:**

**3.** In ancient cultures like that of the Bible, what are some of the rights of sons? What are some of the inheritances of sons? What are some of the responsibilities of sons?

**4.** Is there anything in your experience with your human family that makes it difficult for you to fully understand and believe the depth of your standing with God? If so, what "lesser" story are you believing in that difficulty? We encourage you to bring this need to your community, to encourage you and speak truth in love with you.

**CONSIDER OUR FAMILIAL RELATIONSHIP WITH EACH OTHER:**

**5.** Whether daily, weekly, monthly, annually, or as needed, what are some of the normal things that healthy nuclear families do with each other and/or for each other? What are some similar things you can do, with those in your community?

**6.** What are ways that you've lived out this identity well, toward those in your community? Toward those in your mission field? How have those ways displayed the work of the gospel in your life?

---

### FOR EXTRA STUDY

**7.** In what ways are those in your nuclear family like you, and in what ways aren't they—to the point you don't you even understand each other at times!? How are you stronger—individually and as a family—because of your differences?

**8.** In what ways do you think you live your Family Identity well, and in what ways would you like to grow in living as a better member of God's family—toward God, your community, and your mission field—even if it takes discomfort and/or sacrifice? How can you ask those in your community to help you?

**9.** What questions or ideas from this week's study do you have that you want to discuss when you meet with your faith community?

# PRAY

WEEK 3, DAY 4

*Knowing that we're dependent on God to produce any good fruit in us, spend today walking through the following prayer exercises related to this week's theme.*

## PRAYING THE PSALMS

The Psalms teach us how to approach God in raw, humble ways, and help us remember the truth of who God objectively is, despite our subjective discomfort or circumstances. Slowly consider the words of the psalm, trying to understand it, lingering over it. Then pray it several times as it is written or in your own words as a prayer to God.

**PSALM 133** *A Song of Ascents. Of David.*

Behold, how good and pleasant it is
when brothers dwell in unity!
It is like the precious oil on the head,
running down on the beard,
on the beard of Aaron,
running down on the collar of his robes!
It is like the dew of Hermon,
which falls on the mountains of Zion!
For there the LORD has commanded the blessing,
life forevermore.

**PSALM 139** *To the choirmaster. A Psalm of David.*

O LORD, you have searched me and known me!
You know when I sit down and when I rise up;
  you discern my thoughts from afar.
You search out my path and my lying down
  and are acquainted with all my ways.
Even before a word is on my tongue,
  behold, O LORD, you know it altogether.
You hem me in, behind and before,
  and lay your hand upon me.
Such knowledge is too wonderful for me;
  it is high; I cannot attain it.

Where shall I go from your Spirit?
  Or where shall I flee from your presence?
If I ascend to heaven, you are there!
  If I make my bed in Sheol, you are there!
If I take the wings of the morning
  and dwell in the uttermost parts of the sea,
even there your hand shall lead me,
  and your right hand shall hold me.
If I say, "Surely the darkness shall cover me,
  and the light about me be night,"
even the darkness is not dark to you;
  the night is bright as the day,
  for darkness is as light with you.

For you formed my inward parts;
  you knitted me together in my mother's womb.
I praise you, for I am fearfully and wonderfully made.
Wonderful are your works;
  my soul knows it very well.
My frame was not hidden from you,
  when I was being made in secret,
  intricately woven in the depths of the earth.
Your eyes saw my unformed substance;
  in your book were written, every one of them,
  the days that were formed for me,
  when as yet there was none of them.

How precious to me are your thoughts, O God!
  How vast is the sum of them!
If I would count them, they are more than the sand.
  I awake, and I am still with you.

Oh that you would slay the wicked, O God!
  O men of blood, depart from me!
They speak against you with malicious intent;
  your enemies take your name in vain.
Do I not hate those who hate you, O LORD?
  And do I not loathe those who rise up against you?
I hate them with complete hatred;
  I count them my enemies.
Search me, O God, and know my heart!
  Try me and know my thoughts!
And see if there be any grievous way in me,
  and lead me in the way everlasting!

## CRAFT YOUR OWN PRAYER

In your own words, spend some intentional time talking to and listening for God along this week's theme. We encourage you to write your prayer, as well as thoughts that come to mind that God might be prompting. Test those thoughts against the truth of Scripture, as well as your community. Here are some things you might pray:

- Thank and praise God the Father for being a perfect, unconditionally-loving Father, God the Son for being a good, sacrificial older brother, and God the Spirit for uniting us in childlike relationship to God.

- Think through those in your community and mission field: thank God for specific ways they're like family to you and show you different aspects of the love of God.

- Confess to God areas of sin, disbelief, or discomfort: maybe it's a hard time viewing him as Father; maybe it's inconvenience or distrust that keeps you from sharing life with others; maybe it's judging people in your community or mission field who aren't like you.

- Look back at your answers to yesterday's questions. As you do, consider what jumps out to you, and ask God to lead you in his ways and truth, to help you see lies or untruths that you're believing about him or yourself, to remind you of his identity and work in and through you, and to redeem or restore any brokenness in those areas.

- Stop to listen, be still and quiet before God, and write down any thoughts that come to mind.

## HISTORIC PRAYER

In closing today's prayer exercises, ponder and pray the prayer below, which is pulled from historic Christian literature, and has been prayed by Jesus's disciples for many, many years.

> ...I bow my knees before the Father, from whom every family in heaven and on earth is named, that according to the riches of his glory he may grant you to be strengthened with power through his Spirit in your inner being, so that Christ may dwell in your hearts through faith—that you, being rooted and grounded in love, may have strength to comprehend with all the saints what is the breadth and length and height and depth, and to know the love of Christ that surpasses knowledge, that you may be filled with all the fullness of God. Now to him who is able to do far more abundantly than all that we ask or think, according to the power at work within us, to him be glory in the church and in Christ Jesus throughout all generations, forever and ever. Amen.

**The Apostle Paul, Ephesians 3:14–20**

# DO

## WEEK 3, DAY 5

*Take some time today, by yourself or with others in your faith community, to carry out the following exercises, as you wrap your life around this week's truth.*

In today's culture, our identities often get confused with the various roles we play.

Think about how backward the world is on this. The world defines people based upon what they do, not who they are. What generally happens when you meet someone for the first time? "Hello, my name is Bill," you say. Then the other person says, "Nice to meet you, Bill." What generally comes next? "So . . . what do you do?" You reply that you're a teacher, a plumber, a doctor, a barista, a banker, or any number of other possible professions. We define people—even ourselves—by what they do, not by who they are. Has anyone ever asked you, after hearing your name, "Who are you?" I've done this. It startles people because they don't tend to know who they are apart from what they do. But we're not human doings. We're human beings.

As we've said, as disciples of Christ, we've each been given a new identity. As we consider our Family Identity this week, we must see that this gospel identity transcends whatever roles we play. For example, we're (Jeff and Ben) both pastors, writers, teachers, residents of a certain city, etc. But we don't get to ignore the fact that we're God's sons, existing in a family of brothers and sisters, when we enter those various roles. Instead, it's *within* those everyday roles that we live out our renewed identities.

**1.** Today we consider how to live out our Family Identity, in the roles we play everyday:

- In the first column below, list some of the normal roles you carry out in everyday life (For example: wife, engineer, landlord, etc.)
- In the second column, define your position toward others in each role (For example: subordinate, peer, authority, etc.)
- In the third column, write some ways you can or do live out your Family Identity toward those you interact with in each role.

- In the fourth column, define how often you've lived out your Family Identity well in that role. (1 = rarely; 2 = sometimes; 3 = more often than not; 4 = regularly)
- In the final column, for any you ranked yourself a "1" or "2," write some reasons it's difficult to live out your Family Identity within each role. Look back to Week One, Day Five and see if any of those reasons are excuses/idols.

| ROLE | POSITION | WAYS TO LIVE AS FAMILY | HOW OFTEN | WHY? |
|---|---|---|---|---|
| *Teacher* | *Authority to students; subordinate to dept. head* | *Lunch w/students/faculty; student meetings; campus activities* | *2* | *Introversion; fear; busy; live far away; don't want wrong impression* |
| | | | | |
| | | | | |
| | | | | |
| | | | | |

**2.** In your own words, explain Family Identity. What does it mean that the gospel calls us into a familial relationship with God and others?

**3.** Write down a few familial things you can do this week with those in your community and your mission field. Then get practical: pick up the phone, get together, and do one or two!

# MEET

## WEEK 3, DAY 6

Start by having someone share their story. The goal in sharing stories is to listen for things to celebrate and thank God for, and to listen for themes or areas of life to ask questions and speak truth in love, as you point each other toward Jesus. After they share, pray for the person who shared and ask who will share next week.

*Based on this week's reading, questions, prayers, and activities, honestly discuss questions like the following with your faith community. The tendency is going to want to stay general: get gritty and specific. Commit to putting your belief into action, by planning one or two specific ways to carry out each. Lovingly speak truth into areas of weakness, and figure out together how to encourage each other to infuse the gospel into this week's regular rhythms. And remember, some of this – maybe most of this – can't be limited to the one "official" meeting of your community each week, and this discussion is simply acknowledging who you are personally, as a redeemed follower of Jesus, as you do life together.*

1. From this week's personal preparation, what stood out to you? What was new? What was exciting/hopeful?

2. From this week's personal preparation, is there anything you're confused by/have questions about? What was difficult to read/ponder?

**3.** As disciples of Jesus, how does the gospel call us to be a family? Why is this a vital element of living out our faith in the everyday stuff of life?

**4.** As a community, are there ways we can celebrate God's work in helping us live out this identity well? (For example: how well do we know each other and things in each other's lives, how often do we see each other, how do we love, bless, and serve each other?)

**5.** Using those same criteria, how can we celebrate ways God's led our community to live out our Family Identity in and toward those in our mission field?

**6.** Are there areas we need to grow together, in living out this identity? As we worked through this week's content, what are some ways we came up with by which we might help each other live as family better than we are now?

**7.** Does anyone need help with the things you wrote down on Day 5, knowing how to live out this identity in a certain role, or coming up with familial things we can do together? What do you need from our community to help carry these out, and how can we encourage each other to do them well?

**8.** Is there anything we've discussed tonight that anyone wants to commit to follow-up on or do together in the coming week or beyond? Why or why not?

⊙ *Close your meeting in prayer.*

# REST

## WEEK 3, DAY 7

Knowing we're all busy, and that we all get behind, one day each week doesn't have specific assignments. It's simply a "floating day off" to encourage you to rest and dwell on this week's theme. This day to rest and recreate is designed to break up your week, and to remind you of God's truth and promises: He is sufficient for our every need, we rely on His power and leading to accomplish anything good, we don't have to work to earn his approval, and He is in control regardless of our action or inaction.

WEEK 4

NEW IDENTITY

# Servant

# START

## WEEK 4, DAY 1

*Prayerfully and thoughtfully read this week's reading (or read chapter 13 of* Saturate*). As you read, circle, underline, write in the margins, and interact with concepts or ideas that are new, difficult, inspiring, etc.*

This is the second of three weeks in which we're considering our gospel identities. It's important to remember that our identity informs everything we do, and our identity is founded on who God is and his work in us. Because of the gospel, our new identities are as family, servants, and missionaries. Last week we talked about our Family Identity. This week we consider our Servant Identity.

### WE ARE SERVANTS: BAPTIZED INTO THE NAME OF THE SON (THE KING)

In the beginning, God gave Adam and Eve rule and reign over all the earth. God made them in his image to be a constant reminder to the entire created world that he is the ultimate ruler over all. Everywhere they went, they were to represent God's rule and reign in all they did. Then, as they had children, who likewise would be image bearers, those children also would be a visible reminder of God's rule and reign. This is why Adam and Eve were to be fruitful, multiply, and fill the earth. God's intent was to fill the earth with his image—his glory on display—so that all of creation would show what he is like. That's saturation.

Who is God? The Ruler. What has he done? He has created vice-regents to submit to his rule and to reign over all of creation. Who are we? We are vice-regents given dominion over the earth. What do we do? We rule on God's behalf like he would.

However, the Evil One tricked Adam and Eve into submitting to him as the ruler of the world instead of God. In that moment, they handed over their authority to Satan, and in exchange, they became his slaves. The father of sin and lies became the god of this world. And all of humanity, from that point on, was born into this reality—slavery to sin and to Satan, the god of this world.

It is very apparent that his rule is rotten. Everything is broken under his authority. Relationships are divided and broken. Families are broken, leaving the fatherless and the widow without families. Hatred toward one another is expressed through slander, gossip, and even murder. Selfishness corrupts everything, leading to greed, poverty, and all kinds of abuse and injustice. And the beautiful world God created for us to enjoy and rule continues to be destroyed through human depravity.

So Jesus came as the new human King we all need. He came to set the captives free and bring about a new kingdom where everything would be restored to its previous place under God's very good rule. Jesus is the new King, the new Adam, sent to establish God's rule and reign over all the earth. Jesus came as a King, but his posture is that of a servant. He did not come to be served, for he needed nothing. He came to serve, because we needed everything he had! And he provided us with everything we need as a servant who laid down his life so we could have life.

## SERVING OUR SERVANT KING

Jesus's servants look around and see where things are not as they ought to be. They know what things should be like because they know the story of God's rule and reign in the first garden and the promise of his rule and reign in the future, garden-like city. When Jesus is King over all and everything is in submission to him, there will be no more sin—no more brokenness, no more sickness, no more pain—and we will all have a Father and brothers and sisters. We will all have plenty, and no one will go without. Children will get to have parties. And Jesus will be at the center of it all.

Look around you. Consider where God has placed you and others with you. Does it look like Jesus's kingdom? Are the hungry fed, the naked clothed, the broken brought to health, the disconnected included in families, and the captives set free to fully live? If we are servants of Jesus, we are in the place where he has put us in order to serve others as he served us. He wants people to experience what life can be like in his kingdom through his body, the church. As his body, we give tangible expression to what Jesus is like. He wants people to taste and see, through our actions of love, that he is very good and his kingdom is amazing, so that, after experiencing it, they will want to be with him forever in his kingdom.

Additionally, God intends to saturate not just our leisure hours and weekends with the good news of Jesus. He also intends to saturate our work hours by leading us to serve and worship him while we work. Can you imagine what it would look like if you saw every workday as a worship service? How would you work differently? How would you care for your fellow employees? What if, like Jesus, you and I were more committed to the welfare of others than to our own promotions?

As we serve others as Jesus served us, and work unto the Lord at our workplaces, we bring the experience of Jesus's kingdom into the world. That's what his servants do in their homes, neighborhoods, workplaces, and cities. We do it all so people can experience the greatness of our Servant King and come to him in order to be set free to serve him with all of their hearts and lives as well.

Baptized into the name of the Son, we are his servants. Therefore, we serve the least of the people of the world just as he served us.

## DAY 1: QUESTIONS TO CONSIDER

1. What are some of the ways God the Father, God the Son, and God the Spirit serve each other, serve God's creation, and serve humanity?

2. What are some of the ways God's people serve God, serve God's creation, and serve other people?

3. What's your "gut reaction" to the term "servant"? If it's a negative reaction, what cultural influences have made it negative in your mind? How should our new identity in the gospel lead us to greater humility?

# READ

## WEEK 4, DAY 2

*Prayerfully and thoughtfully read the biblical texts below, then spend a few moments reflecting on the truths therein by answering the questions at the end.*

Where do you see the Bible speak of the depth of our relationships, whether explicitly mentioned, implied by actions, or as simply necessary to rightly understand the passage?

◘ Box areas you see the servant relationship between God the Father, Son, and Spirit

○ Circle areas you see God serving his creation and people

★ Star areas you see God's people serving God and serving each other

### 1 CHRONICLES 29:10-14

Therefore David blessed the LORD in the presence of all the assembly. And David said: "Blessed are you, O LORD, the God of Israel our father, forever and ever. Yours, O LORD, is the greatness and the power and the glory and the victory and the majesty, for all that is in the heavens and in the earth is yours. Yours is the kingdom, O LORD, and you are exalted as head above all. Both riches and honor come from you, and you rule over all. In your hand are power and might, and in your hand it is to make great and to give strength to all. And now we thank you, our God, and praise your glorious name. But who am I, and what is my people, that we should be able thus to offer willingly? For all things come from you, and of your own have we given you..."

### MATTHEW 25:31-46

"When the Son of Man comes in his glory, and all the angels with him, then he will sit on his glorious throne. Before him will be gathered all the nations, and he will separate people one from another as a shepherd separates the sheep from the goats. And he will place the sheep on his right, but the goats on the left. Then the King will say to those on his right, 'Come, you who are blessed by my Father, inherit the kingdom prepared for you from the foundation of the world. For I was hungry and you gave me food, I was thirsty and you gave me drink, I was a stranger and you welcomed me, I was naked and you clothed me, I was sick and you visited me, I was in prison and you came to me.' Then the righteous will answer him, saying, 'Lord, when did we see you hungry and feed you, or thirsty and give you drink? And when did we see you a stranger and welcome you, or naked and clothe you? And when did we see you sick or in prison and visit you?' And the King will answer them, 'Truly, I say to you, as you did it to one of the least of these my brothers, you did it to me.'

"Then he will say to those on his left, 'Depart from me, you cursed, into the eternal fire prepared for the devil and his angels. For I was hungry and you gave me no food, I was thirsty and you gave me no drink, I was a stranger and you did not welcome me, naked and you did not clothe me, sick and in prison and you did not visit me.' Then they also will answer, saying, 'Lord, when did we see you hungry or thirsty or a stranger or naked or sick or in prison, and did not minister to you?' Then he will answer them, saying, 'Truly, I say to you, as you did not do it to one of the least of these, you did not do it to me.' And these will go away into eternal punishment, but the righteous into eternal life."

### LUKE 19:8-10

Zacchaeus stood and said to the Lord, "Behold, Lord, the half of my goods I give to the poor. And if I have defrauded anyone of anything, I restore it fourfold." And Jesus said to him, "Today salvation has come to this house, since he also is a son of Abraham. For the Son of Man came to seek and to save the lost."

### ROMANS 8:26-27

Likewise the Spirit helps us in our weakness. For we do not know what to pray for as we ought, but the Spirit himself intercedes for us with groanings too deep for words. And he who searches hearts knows what is the mind of the Spirit, because the Spirit intercedes for the saints according to the will of God.

### 1 CORINTHIANS 12:4-13

Now there are varieties of gifts, but the same Spirit; and there are varieties of service, but the same Lord; and there are varieties of activities, but it is the same God who empowers them all in everyone. To each is given the manifestation of the Spirit for the common good. For to one is given through the Spirit the utterance of wisdom, and to another the utterance of knowledge according to the same Spirit, to another faith by the same Spirit, to another gifts of healing by the one Spirit, to another the working of miracles, to another prophecy, to another the ability to distinguish between spirits, to another various kinds of tongues, to another the interpretation of tongues. All these are empowered by one and the same Spirit, who apportions to each one individually as he wills. For just as the body is one and has many members, and all the members of the body, though many, are one body, so it is with Christ. For in one Spirit we were all baptized into one body—Jews or Greeks, slaves or free—and all were made to drink of one Spirit.

### PHILIPPIANS 2:5-11

Have this mind among yourselves, which is yours in Christ Jesus, who, though he was in the form of God, did not count equality with God a thing to be grasped, but emptied himself, by taking the form of a servant, being born in the likeness of men. And being found in human form, he humbled himself by becoming obedient to the point of death, even death on a cross. Therefore God has highly exalted him and bestowed on him the name that is above every name, so that at the name of Jesus every knee should bow, in heaven and on earth and under the earth, and every tongue confess that Jesus Christ is Lord, to the glory of God the Father.

### 1 PETER 2:13-18

Be subject for the Lord's sake to every human institution, whether it be to the emperor as supreme, or to governors as sent by him to punish those who do evil and to praise those who do good. For this is the will of God, that by doing good you should put to silence the ignorance of foolish people. Live as people who are free, not using your freedom as a cover-up for evil, but living as servants of God. Honor everyone. Love the brotherhood. Fear God. Honor the emperor. Servants, be subject to your masters with all respect, not only to the good and gentle but also to the unjust.

---

**FOR MORE:**

Matthew 5:43-48 / John 13:1-17 / Acts 17:24-25 / 2 Corinthians 4:5-6 / Colossians 3:18-4:1

## DAY 2: QUESTIONS TO CONSIDER

Answer these questions as you think about what you saw in today's verses:

1. What themes jumped out to you as you reviewed these texts?

2. Look back through these verses: what are some of the things that the biblical authors describe God's people doing as they served God and others?

3. Matthew 25 describes serving others as a means of serving our King Jesus: how does this inform our motive and posture in loving, serving, and blessing others? Why is it sometimes difficult to see serving other people as a means of serving God?

**4.** If, as stated in a few of the verses above, God doesn't need to be served, why do we serve? How do we reflect the gospel as we serve?

There are plenty of stories, verses, and instances in the Bible where God's people didn't rest in the truths of the gospel. Think about what you know of the Bible and Story of God and answer the following questions. If you need a jumpstart, consider these passages: 2 Kings 17; Ezekiel 34; Mark 9:33-38; 1 Corinthians 12:12-26; 1 Peter 5:1-5.

**5.** Who are some of the people described throughout the Bible as adopting a posture of non-humility and authoritarian rule instead of servant leadership? How are they described in the Bible?

**6.** What examples can you think of where people decided they didn't need each other's gifts and service? How are those people described in the Bible?

# THINK

## WEEK 4, DAY 3

*Knowing that each week builds on previous weeks, prayerfully and honestly work through these questions and exercises, in light of previous weeks' and this week's themes.*

Consider how the Servant Identity plays out in your mind and life by asking yourself the following questions in light of this week's theme. Don't feel like you need to answer every question: instead, choose those that most resonate with you, that you feel God the Spirit speaking to you through, or maybe those that are most challenging to you—either way, we encourage you to answer at least one question from each section, and to write down your answers.

### DAY 3: QUESTIONS TO CONSIDER

**In addition to the answers given to these questions in Day 1's reading, consider these aspects of God's story, thinking specifically in terms of servanthood:**

1. Who is God and what has he done (in regards to himself, his creation, and service)?
   *As part of your answer to this question, think of specific ways God has served you, and the way that his service impacts you.*

2. Who are we and what do we do (in regards to God, his creation, and service)?

## CONSIDERING OUR SERVANT IDENTITY BETWEEN GOD AND OURSELVES:

**3.** Compare Jesus's kingship with most rulers in history: what difference does it make that Jesus came as a humble servant rather than an authoritarian tyrant (even though he, above any other ruler on earth, has the right to full authority!)?

**4.** What are some specific ways that you can "present your bodies as a living sacrifice, holy and acceptable to God, which is your spiritual worship" (Rom. 12:1), directly to God?

## CONSIDERING OUR SERVANT IDENTITY LIVED OUT TOWARD OTHERS:

**5.** Is it difficult to think of ways to specifically serve God, without involving service and blessing to others? Do you think that's intentional on God's part? Why or why not?

**6.** Consider where God has placed you and those with you: Are the hungry fed, the naked clothed, the broken brought to health, the disconnected included in families, and the captives set free to fully live? How do each of these images relate to our Servant Identity?

---

### FOR EXTRA STUDY

**7.** Colossians calls us to do our work "as for the Lord and not for men." What would it look like if you saw every workday as a worship service? How would you work differently? Whether you're a CEO, a stay-at-home parent, an artist, or whatever else, how would you care for your fellow co-workers, or those for/with whom you labor?

**8.** In what ways do you think you live your Servant Identity well, and in what ways would you like to grow in living as a better servant of God—toward God, your community, and your mission field—even if it takes discomfort and/or sacrifice? How can you ask those in your community to help you?

**9.** What questions or ideas do you have from this week's study that you want to discuss when you meet with your faith community?

# PRAY

## WEEK 4, DAY 4

*Knowing that we're dependent on God to produce any good fruit in us, spend today walking through the following prayer exercises related to this week's theme.*

### PRAYING THE PSALMS

The Psalms teach us how to approach God in raw, humble ways, and help us remember the truth of who God objectively is, despite our subjective discomfort or circumstances. Slowly consider the words of the psalm, trying to understand it, lingering over it. Then pray it several times as it is written or in your own words as a prayer to God.

**PSALM 23** *A Psalm of David.*

The LORD is my shepherd; I shall not want.
He makes me lie down in green pastures.
He leads me beside still waters.
He restores my soul.
He leads me in paths of righteousness
for his name's sake.

Even though I walk through the valley of the
shadow of death,
I will fear no evil,
for you are with me;
your rod and your staff,
they comfort me.

You prepare a table before me
in the presence of my enemies;
you anoint my head with oil;
my cup overflows.
Surely goodness and mercy shall follow me
all the days of my life,
and I shall dwell in the house of the LORD
forever.

**PSALM 103** *Of David.*

Bless the LORD, O my soul,
and all that is within me,
bless his holy name!
Bless the LORD, O my soul,
and forget not all his benefits,
who forgives all your iniquity,
who heals all your diseases,
who redeems your life from the pit,
who crowns you with steadfast love and mercy,
who satisfies you with good
so that your youth is renewed like the eagle's.

The LORD works righteousness
and justice for all who are oppressed.
He made known his ways to Moses,
his acts to the people of Israel.
The LORD is merciful and gracious,
slow to anger and abounding in steadfast love.
He will not always chide,
nor will he keep his anger forever.
He does not deal with us according to our sins,
nor repay us according to our iniquities.
For as high as the heavens are above the earth,
so great is his steadfast love toward those who fear him;
as far as the east is from the west,
so far does he remove our transgressions from us.
As a father shows compassion to his children,
so the LORD shows compassion to those who fear him.
For he knows our frame;
he remembers that we are dust.

As for man, his days are like grass;
he flourishes like a flower of the field;
for the wind passes over it, and it is gone,
and its place knows it no more.
But the steadfast love of the LORD is from everlasting
to everlasting on those who fear him,
and his righteousness to children's children,
to those who keep his covenant
and remember to do his commandments.
The LORD has established his throne in the heavens,
and his kingdom rules over all.

Bless the LORD, O you his angels,
you mighty ones who do his word,
obeying the voice of his word!
Bless the LORD, all his hosts,
his ministers, who do his will!
Bless the LORD, all his works,
in all places of his dominion.
Bless the LORD, O my soul!

## CRAFT YOUR OWN PRAYER

In your own words, spend some intentional time talking to and listening for God along this week's theme. We encourage you to write your prayer, as well as thoughts that come to mind that God might be prompting. Test those thoughts against the truth of Scripture, as well as your community. Here are some things you might pray:

- Thank and praise God the Son for being a perfect picture of humility and for carrying out his rule and reign on the earth through the posture of a servant.

- Think through those in your community and mission field: thank God for specific ways they've served you, and show you different aspects of humility, blessing, and sacrifice.

- Confess to God areas of sin, disbelief, or discomfort: maybe you have a hard time accepting the posture of a servant; maybe it's inconvenience or entitlement that keeps you from humbling yourself or considering others' needs; maybe it's judging people in your community or mission field who you think are demanding, selfish, or unworthy of service.

- Look back at your answers to yesterday's questions. As you do, consider what jumps out to you, and ask God to lead you in his ways and truth, to help you see lies or untruths that you're believing about him or yourself, to remind you of his identity and work in and through you, and to redeem or restore any brokenness in those areas.

- Stop to listen, be still and quiet before God, and write down any thoughts that come to mind.

## HISTORIC PRAYER

In closing today's prayer exercises, ponder and pray the prayer below, which is pulled from historic Christian literature, and has been prayed by Jesus's disciples for many, many years.

> Lord, make me an instrument of Your peace. Where there is hatred, let me sow love; where there is injury, pardon; where there is doubt, faith; where there is despair, hope; where there is darkness, light; where there is sadness, joy.
>
> O, Divine Master, grant that I may not so much seek to be consoled as to console; to be understood as to understand; to be loved as to love; For it is in giving that we receive; it is in pardoning that we are pardoned; it is in dying that we are born again to eternal life.

**ST. FRANCIS OF ASSISI**

# DO

## WEEK 4, DAY 5

*Take some time today, by yourself or with others in your faith community, to carry out the following exercises, as you wrap your life around this week's truth.*

Today's "Day 5" follows the same pattern as last week's "Day 5", but with our Servant Identity. To refresh your memory, we're starting with the same words as last week's "Day 5": As we've been talking about, as disciples of Christ we've each been given a new identity: as we consider our Servant Identity this week, we must see that this gospel identity transcends whatever roles we play. But we don't get to ignore the fact that we're servants of King Jesus, committed to serve God by serving those around us, when we enter those various roles. Instead, it's within those everyday roles that we live out our renewed identities.

**1.** Today we consider how to live out our Servant Identity in the roles we play everyday—because it's often those we're around most often who we can serve the most:

- Look back at the everyday roles you wrote last week, and the position toward others in each role. If it would be helpful for you, rewrite those roles in the first column below, and in the second column rewrite your position toward others—this becomes especially important as we consider our Servant Identity! And if you think of additional roles you hadn't written last week, add them to Columns 1 and 2.

- In the third column, especially considering your position toward others, write some ways you can or do live out your Servant Identity toward those you interact with in each role. (For example: how can you use your authority for the benefit of others? How can you submit even if you're not treated fairly? etc.)

- In the fourth column, consider how often you've lived out your Servant Identity well in that role. (1 = rarely; 2 = sometimes; 3 = more often than not; 4 = regularly)

- In the final column, for any you ranked yourself a "1" or "2," write some reasons it's difficult to live out your Servant Identity within each role. Look back to Week One, Day Five and see if any of those reasons are excuses/idols.

| ROLE | POSITION | WAYS TO LIVE AS SERVANT | HOW OFTEN | WHY? |
| --- | --- | --- | --- | --- |
| *Teacher* | *Authority to students; subordinate to dept. head* | *Grade with grace, round up! Meet at inconvenient times. Go above & beyond my duty* | *2* | *Entitlement; I use my age & experience to get my way & be served* |
| | | | | |
| | | | | |
| | | | | |
| | | | | |

2. In your own words, explain the Servant Identity: what does it mean that the gospel calls us into a servant relationship toward God and those he puts around us?

3. Write down a few things you can do this week to serve specific people in your community and your mission field. Then get practical: get supplies if needed, head their way, and do one or two!

## WEEK 4, DAY 6

Start by having someone share their story. The goal in sharing stories is to listen for things to celebrate and thank God for, and to listen for themes or areas of life to ask questions and speak truth in love, as you point each other toward Jesus. After they share, pray for the person who shared and ask who will share next week.

*Based on this week's reading, questions, prayers, and activities, honestly discuss questions like the following with your faith community. The tendency is going to want to stay general: get gritty and specific. Commit to putting your belief into action, by planning one or two specific ways to carry out each. Lovingly speak truth into areas of weakness, and figure out together how to encourage each other to infuse the gospel into this week's regular rhythms. And remember, some of this – maybe most of this – can't be limited to the one "official" meeting of your community each week, and this discussion is simply acknowledging who you are personally, as a redeemed follower of Jesus, as you do life together.*

**1.** From this week's personal preparation, what stood out to you? What was new? What was exciting/hopeful?

**2.** From this week's personal preparation, is there anything you're confused by/have questions about? What was difficult to read/ponder?

3. As disciples of Jesus, how does the gospel call us to be servants? Why is this a vital element of living out our faith in the everyday stuff of life?

4. As a community, are there ways we can celebrate God's work in helping us live out this identity well? (For example: how well do we inconvenience ourselves for each other, how often do we see, bless, and help each other, how do we express and meet needs well?)

5. Using those same criteria, how can we celebrate ways God's led our community to live out our Servant Identity in and toward those in our mission field?

6. Are there areas we need to grow together in living out this identity? As we worked through this week's content, what are some ways we came up with by which we might help each other live as servants better than we are?

7. Does anyone need help with the things you wrote down on Day 5, knowing how to live out this identity in a certain role, or coming up with servant-driven things we can do together? What do you need from our community to help carry these out, and/or how can we encourage each other to do them well?

8. Is there anything we've discussed tonight that anyone wants to commit to follow-up on or do together in the coming week or beyond? Why or why not?

⊙ *Close your meeting in prayer.*

# REST

## WEEK 4, DAY 7

Knowing we're all busy, and that we all get behind, one day each week doesn't have specific assignments. It's simply a "floating day off" to encourage you to rest and dwell on this week's theme. This day to rest and recreate is designed to break up your week, and to remind you of God's truth and promises: He is sufficient for our every need, we rely on His power and leading to accomplish anything good, we don't have to work to earn his approval, and He is in control regardless of our action or inaction.

# WEEK 5

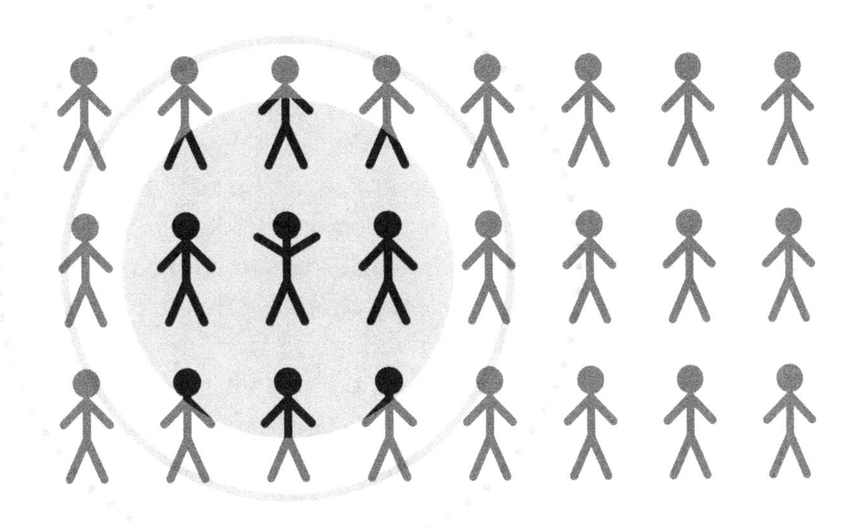

NEW IDENTITY

# Missionary

# START

## WEEK 5, DAY 1

For video and additional resources pertaining to Week 5, visit:

www.saturatetheworld.com/fg/week5

*Prayerfully and thoughtfully read this week's reading (or read chapter 14 of Saturate). As you read, circle, underline, write in the margins, and interact with concepts or ideas that are new, difficult, inspiring, etc.*

This is the last of three weeks in which we're considering our gospel identities. As a reminder, our identity informs everything we do, and our identity is founded on who God is and his work in us. Because of the gospel, our new identities are as family, servants, and missionaries. Two weeks ago, we talked about family, last week we considered servant, and this week we wrap up our identity conversations by consider our Missionary Identity.

### WE ARE MISSIONARIES: BAPTIZED INTO THE NAME OF THE HOLY SPIRIT

God dwelt with Adam and Eve in the garden and gave them a mission to accomplish with his presence and help. But when they rebelled against him, he drove them out.

He dwelt with his people Israel while they traveled in the desert. Moses told God he would not go to the Promised Land unless God went with them. He asked God: "How shall it be known that I have found favor in your sight, I and your people? Is it not in your going with us, so that we are distinct, I and your people, from every other people on the face of the earth?" (Ex. 33:16). Moses knew that it was God with them that gave them their identity, purpose, and power. Eventually, God instructed his people to build him a dwelling place (the tabernacle), where he would dwell with them when they paused in their travels. When they finally arrived in the land, they eventually built a temple as a permanent place of dwelling for the Lord. Before God came to dwell in the tabernacle and temple, both had to be purified by the shedding of the blood of an innocent animal. Once the tabernacle or temple and its articles of worship were purified, God dwelt there.

However, a better dwelling place was to come. God wanted to dwell not only with his people. He wanted to dwell in his people. So he sent the Son—Jesus. Jesus was baptized by John in the Jordan River before he began his earthly ministry. When he came out of the waters of baptism, the Spirit descended upon him in the form of a dove and the Father said, "This is my beloved Son, with whom I am well pleased" (Matt. 3:17).

## DISPLAYING AND DECLARING THE GOOD NEWS

Jesus was then filled with and led by the Holy Spirit to be tempted by the Devil. Just as Adam and Eve were tempted, so Jesus also had to be tempted in order to accomplish what Adam and Eve could not. [By the power of that same Spirit,] Jesus preached with incredible authority and made some audacious claims, and went on to heal the sick, raise the dead, and cast out demons, all by the power of the Holy Spirit. Jesus displayed the good news of the kingdom.

In the book of Acts, Luke gives us a very detailed account of Jesus's ministry as Jesus was filled with and led by the Holy Spirit. Then he gives a detailed account of the early church's ministry as they were filled with and led by the Holy Spirit. Both ministries look the same because it was the same Spirit. Jesus told the disciples to wait in Jerusalem for the Holy Spirit, "for John baptized with water, but you will be baptized with the Holy Spirit not many days from now" (Acts 1:4-5). Then he said to them, "You will receive power when the Holy Spirit has come upon you, and you will be my witnesses in Jerusalem and in all Judea and Samaria, and to the ends of the earth" (v. 8). "As the Father has sent me, even so I am sending you."

When the Spirit filled the first disciples, all 120 of them, men and women, young and old, proclaimed the mighty deeds of God in languages all of the visitors to Jerusalem could understand. Then Peter got up to explain it, and in the power of the Holy Spirit, he preached a message through which more than three thousand people came to faith in Jesus and were added to the family of God in one day (Acts 2). It wasn't an incredibly well-written and well-prepared message. It was a Spirit-empowered message that led to thousands becoming disciples of Jesus.

## ALWAYS ON MISSION

You and I, if we have the Spirit of Christ, have the same power to proclaim the good news of Jesus as Jesus did. You don't need a seminary degree or a Bible school education. You don't need a title or position. Jesus's disciples had none of these. But they had been with Jesus, and Jesus was with them by his Spirit. He is with you, too.

Let's think through our four questions again. Who is God? He is Spirit. What has he done? He sent and empowered Jesus the Son to take on flesh and to seek and save what was lost. Who are we? We are missionaries, sent and empowered by the same Spirit. If we believe this, what do we do? We make disciples of Jesus through proclaiming the gospel in the power of the Spirit. If you are a child of God and a servant of King Jesus, you have been sent into the world as his missionary with the same Spirit that sent and empowered Jesus.

You are Jesus's missionaries, sent with his Spirit to proclaim the good news of Jesus with authority and boldness. That is why Jesus gave you his Spirit—so you could be his witnesses (Acts 1:8). Charles Spurgeon said, "Every Christian is either a missionary or an imposter." Everywhere you go, whatever you do, you are a missionary sent by Jesus to love like Jesus, overcome sin like Jesus, proclaim the gospel like Jesus, and see people's lives changed by the power of the Spirit that raised Jesus from the dead. You are always on mission. Every part of your life, every activity and event, is part of Jesus's mission to make disciples.

## WHO WE ARE, BECAUSE OF WHO GOD IS

If you're a follower of Jesus, who believes the gospel is the central motivation in your life, then your first priority in life is to live as a disciple who makes disciples. This means more than just "making converts." It means living out your everyday life and rhythms[6] in a way that encourages other followers of Jesus in areas of their life where they don't functionally live out God's gospel story. *AND* it means living out your everyday life and rhythms in a way that introduces not-yet-believers to God's gospel story in real, tangible ways. That's part of "the good works [God] prepared beforehand" (Ephesians 2:10) and "the work of ministry" your leaders equip you for (Ephesians 4:12). Read Jesus's own words to his followers: "As the Father has sent me, even so I am sending you" (John 20:21).

Remember, you are not alone on this mission. Jesus goes with you everywhere because his Spirit is in you to empower you to be his representative in the world. He wants to saturate your world in Word and deed by his presence at work in and through you by his Spirit.

We are the Father's family; therefore, we love others like he loved us.

We are servants of Christ; therefore, we serve the least of these as he served us.

We are missionaries filled and empowered by the same Spirit that was in Jesus; therefore, we are always on mission to proclaim the good news of Jesus.

Whatever he has done to us, he now wants to do through us to others.

---

**6.** 'Rhythms,' which we'll dive into deeper starting next week, are things that humans in every culture and across history do, whether daily, weekly, or monthly: every culture eats, celebrates, shares stories, listens, blesses, and re-creates (which involves both resting and creating). As we learn to live our everyday lives with gospel intentionality, these rhythms—in addition to others in your personal routine—are common ways we can display our gospel identities, and can show what it looks like to follow Jesus in the normal stuff of life

## DAY 1: QUESTIONS TO CONSIDER

1. What's your first impression when you think of the word "missionary"? Is it difficult for you to consider yourself God's missionary, in your hometown and everyday life—instead of just occasionally on trips to other cities or nations? Why?

2. What are some of the ways God the Father is shown as a missionary God, God the Son as being the Sent One, and God the Spirit indwelling us to carry out God's mission?

3. Is it difficult to believe that God the Spirit, who enacted and led Jesus in his power and ministry, dwells in you and will enact and lead you to the same things? If so, why is it difficult?

# READ

## WEEK 5, DAY 2

*Prayerfully and thoughtfully read the biblical texts below, then spend a few moments reflecting on the truths therein by answering the questions at the end.*

Where do you see the Bible speak of the depth of our relationships, whether explicitly mentioned, implied by actions, or as simply necessary to rightly understand the passage?

- ◘ Box areas you see God as a missionary/sending God
- ○ Circle terms/"titles" that refer to the Missionary Identity of God's people
- ★ Star areas you see God's people carrying out God's mission, by God's power

### ISAIAH 6:8

And I heard the voice of the Lord saying, "Whom shall I send, and who will go for us?" Then I said, "Here I am! Send me."

### JEREMIAH 29:4-7

Thus says the LORD of hosts, the God of Israel, to all the exiles whom I have sent into exile from Jerusalem to Babylon: "Build houses and live in them; plant gardens and eat their produce. Take wives and have sons and daughters; take wives for your sons, and give your daughters in marriage, that they may bear sons and daughters; multiply there, and do not decrease. But seek the welfare of the city where I have sent you into exile, and pray to the LORD on its behalf, for in its welfare you will find your welfare."

### MATTHEW 9:10-13

And as Jesus reclined at table in the house, behold, many tax collectors and sinners came and were reclining with Jesus and his disciples. And when the Pharisees saw this, they said to his disciples, "Why does your teacher eat with tax collectors and sinners?" But when he heard it, he said, "Those who are well have no need of a physician, but those who are sick. Go and learn what this means, 'I desire mercy, and not sacrifice.' For I came not to call the righteous, but sinners."

### LUKE 4:17-21

And the scroll of the prophet Isaiah was given to him. He unrolled the scroll and found the place where it was written,

"The Spirit of the Lord is upon me,
because he has anointed me
to proclaim good news to the poor.
He has sent me to proclaim liberty to the captives
and recovering of sight to the blind,
to set at liberty those who are oppressed,
to proclaim the year of the Lord's favor."

And he rolled up the scroll and gave it back to the attendant and sat down. And the eyes of all in the synagogue were fixed on him. And he began to say to them, "Today this Scripture has been fulfilled in your hearing."

### JOHN 17:14-19

I have given them your word, and the world has hated them because they are not of the world, just as I am not of the world. I do not ask that you take them out of the world, but that you keep them from the evil one. They are not of the world, just as I am not of the world. Sanctify them in the truth; your word is truth. As you sent me into the world, so I have sent them into the world. And for their sake I consecrate myself, that they also may be sanctified in truth.

### 2 CORINTHIANS 5:16-21

From now on, therefore, we regard no one according to the flesh. Even though we once regarded Christ according to the flesh, we regard him thus no longer. Therefore, if anyone is in Christ, he is a new creation. The old has passed away; behold, the new has come. All this is from God, who through Christ reconciled us to himself and gave us the ministry of reconciliation; that is, in Christ God was reconciling the world to himself, not counting their trespasses against them, and entrusting to us the message of reconciliation. Therefore, we are ambassadors for Christ, God making his appeal through us. We implore you on behalf of Christ, be reconciled to God. For our sake he made him to be sin who knew no sin, so that in him we might become the righteousness of God.

### 1 PETER 2:9-12

But you are a chosen race, a royal priesthood, a holy nation, a people for his own possession, that you may proclaim the excellencies of him who called you out of darkness into his marvelous light. Once you were not a people, but now you are God's people; once you had not received mercy, but now you have received mercy. Beloved, I urge you as sojourners and exiles to abstain from the passions of the flesh, which wage war against your soul. Keep your conduct among the Gentiles honorable, so that when they speak against you as evildoers, they may see your good deeds and glorify God on the day of visitation.

---

**FOR MORE:**

Matthew 28:18-20 / John 1:1-4, 14 / Acts 1:4-5, 8 / Galatians 5:19-6:2 / 1 Thessalonians 2:8

## DAY 2: QUESTIONS TO CONSIDER

Answer these questions as you think about what you saw in today's verses:

1. What themes jumped out to you as you examined these texts?

2. Look back through these verses: what are some of the things that the biblical authors describe God's people doing that display and declare the gospel?

3. If God works through us—his people—why is the Holy Spirit such a vital part of God's mission, mentioned often in the context of our Missionary Identity?

**4.** In John 17, Jesus specifically prays that God *won't* remove us from this world, but instead sends us into it. How does that impact your view of God, his mission, and our role in it?

There are plenty of stories, verses, and instances in the Bible where God's people didn't rest in the truths of the gospel. Think about what you know of the Bible and Story of God and answer the following questions. If you need a jumpstart, consider these passages: Jonah 4; Mark 10:17-39; Acts 15:1-29; 2 Corinthians 11:1-6; Galatians 1:6-24.

**5.** Who are some of the people described throughout the Bible as denying their Missionary Identity or rejecting those who weren't yet God's people (Israel in the Old Testament; the Church in the New Testament)? How are they described in the Bible?

**6.** What other gospels—what lesser stories, false saviors or identities, and alternate forms of "good news"—do we see proclaimed throughout the Bible? Why is it so easy for people (both then and today) to put their hope in other things, and "declare the excellencies" of those things more than God's?

# THINK

## WEEK 5, DAY 3

*Knowing that each week builds on previous weeks, prayerfully and honestly work through these questions and exercises, in light of previous weeks' and this week's themes.*

As Jesus and his followers carried out God's mission, we see them consistently model things that often make us uncomfortable:

- **Jesus *actually* went into the darkness:** Jesus never crossed the line into sin, but he ate with sinners, went into forbidden leper colonies, ate and drank, and broke "religious-looking" rules and rituals that his culture valued. If we're going to be light to the darkness, we have to get out of our own comfort zones and religious-looking rules, and be willing to go into the darkness!

- **Jesus surrounded himself with people who weren't like each other:** Among his apostles were a tax collector and a zealot (who hated tax collectors). There was a doctor and a fisherman. There was a prostitute. If the image of the Church is one of "family," then making disciples includes being surrounded by folks—both believers and not-yet-believers—who aren't like you, who you might not understand! But you devote your life to them because of the deeper bond of Jesus and his mission.

- **Jesus rearranged his followers' lives:** From calling his first disciples—"Come, follow me, and I will make you fishers of men" (Matt. 4:19)—to his call to "deny himself and take up his cross and follow me" Mark 8:34), Jesus asks his followers to do literally everything they can in order to devote themselves to his calling. Sometimes this looked like embedding themselves into a new mission field; other times it looked like changing careers for the sake of God's call; still other times it meant suffering and persecution. The tough truth is that if you call yourself a follower of Jesus, *you actually have to follow him*: to model your life after him and do what he says to do!

## DAY 3: QUESTIONS TO CONSIDER

Consider how the Missionary Identity plays out in your mind and life, by asking yourself the following questions in light of this week's theme. Don't feel like you need to answer every question: instead, choose those that most resonate with you, that you feel God the Spirit speaking to you through, or maybe those that are most challenging to you—either way, we encourage you to answer at least one question from each question, and to write down your answers.

**In addition to the answers given to these questions in Day 1's reading, consider these aspects of God's story, thinking specifically in terms of God's mission:**

1. Who is God and what has he done (in regards to himself, his creation, and his mission)?
   *[As you answer this question, think about God's mission to you personally, as well as his worldwide and history-long mission]*

2. Who are we and what do we do (in regards to God, his creation, and his mission)?

### CONSIDERING THE MISSION OF GOD IN GENERAL:

3. What are some of the ways that Jesus broke religious norms and "went into the darkness" for the sake of "seeking and saving the lost"? How should this influence us?

**4.** In Jonah, Romans, and other places in the Bible, we see that "salvation is of the Lord." At times, however, Christians seem to attempt to play the role of the Holy Spirit. Have you ever done this? What difference does relying on, being led by, and being filled with the Spirit make in our life and mission?

**CONSIDERING YOUR INVOLVEMENT IN GOD'S MISSION:**

**5.** If you were asked "To whom has God sent you on mission?" or "What is your defined mission field?" how would you answer? What are some ways God has rearranged your life to the location, rhythms, and routines of that mission field? If you don't have specific people, or a group of people toward whom you're involved in God's mission, why not?

**6.** If God has only called some of Jesus's disciples into church leadership (and even fewer into regular preaching roles) and has only gifted some as evangelists, but still charges every Christian with the Great Commission, in what ways has he designed mission to be carried out, other than Sunday preaching and formal gospel presentations, apologetics, etc.?

## FOR EXTRA STUDY

7. Look back over Days 1 and 2: write down specific things that God the Spirit did in and through Jesus, and promises to do in and through his disciples (including us). What's comforting about your list? What's difficult?

8. In what ways do you think you live your Missionary Identity well, and in what ways would you like to grow in living as a better servant of God —toward God, your community, and your mission field—even if it takes discomfort and/or sacrifice? How can you ask those in your community to help you?

9. What questions or ideas do you have from this week's study that you want to discuss when you meet with your faith community?

# PRAY

## WEEK 5, DAY 4

*Knowing that we're dependent on God to produce any good fruit in us, spend today walking through the following prayer exercises related to this week's theme.*

### PRAYING THE PSALMS

The Psalms teach us how to approach God in raw, humble ways, and help us remember the truth of who God objectively is, despite our subjective discomfort or circumstances. Slowly consider the words of the psalm, trying to understand it, lingering over it. Then pray it several times as it is written or in your own words as a prayer to God.

**PSALM 67** *To the choirmaster: with stringed instruments. A Psalm. A Song.*

May God be gracious to us and bless us
and make his face to shine upon us, Selah
that your way may be known on earth,
your saving power among all nations.
Let the peoples praise you, O God;
let all the peoples praise you!

Let the nations be glad and sing for joy,
for you judge the peoples with equity
and guide the nations upon earth. Selah
Let the peoples praise you, O God;
let all the peoples praise you!

The earth has yielded its increase;
God, our God, shall bless us.
God shall bless us;
let all the ends of the earth fear him!

## PSALM 96

Oh sing to the LORD a new song;
 sing to the LORD, all the earth!
Sing to the LORD, bless his name;
 tell of his salvation from day to day.
Declare his glory among the nations,
 his marvelous works among all the peoples!
For great is the LORD, and greatly to be praised;
 he is to be feared above all gods.
For all the gods of the peoples are worthless idols,
 but the LORD made the heavens.
Splendor and majesty are before him;
 strength and beauty are in his sanctuary.

Ascribe to the LORD, O families of the peoples,
 ascribe to the LORD glory and strength!
Ascribe to the LORD the glory due his name;
 bring an offering, and come into his courts!
Worship the LORD in the splendor of holiness;
 tremble before him, all the earth!

Say among the nations, "The LORD reigns!
 Yes, the world is established; it shall never be moved;
 he will judge the peoples with equity."

Let the heavens be glad, and let the earth rejoice;
 let the sea roar, and all that fills it;
 let the field exult, and everything in it!
Then shall all the trees of the forest sing for joy
 before the LORD, for he comes,
 for he comes to judge the earth.
He will judge the world in righteousness,
 and the peoples in his faithfulness.

## CRAFT YOUR OWN PRAYER

In your own words, spend some intentional time talking to and listening for God along this week's theme. We encourage you to write your prayer, as well as thoughts that come to mind that God might be prompting. Test those thoughts against the truth of Scripture, as well as your community. Here are some things you might pray:

- Thank and praise God the Son for your own salvation: consider the people God has used as missionaries in your own life, and the circumstances he orchestrated to bring you to reliance on him.

- Pray for individuals in your community and mission field: pray for God to open the eyes of those who don't yet know him, and for wisdom and discernment for your community, in winsomely, humbly, and boldly displaying and declaring the gospel to those around you.

- Confess to God areas of sin, disbelief, or discomfort: maybe you're insecure about sharing the gospel; maybe it's inconvenience or fear that keeps you from living out God's Missionary Identity; maybe it's filling your time with other things and ignoring others.

- Look back at your answers to yesterday's questions. As you do, consider what jumps out to you, and ask God to lead you in his ways and truth, to help you see lies or untruths that you're believing about him or yourself, to remind you of his identity and work in and through you, and to redeem or restore any brokenness in those areas.

- Stop to listen, be still and quiet before God, and write down any thoughts that come to mind.

## HISTORIC PRAYER

In closing today's prayer exercises, ponder and pray the prayer below, which is pulled from historic Christian literature, and has been prayed by Jesus's disciples for many, many years.

May the Strength of God guide us.
May the Power of God preserve us.
May the Wisdom of God instruct us.
May the Hand of God protect us.
May the Way of God direct us.
May the Shield of God defend us.
May the Angels of God guard us.
- Against the snares of the evil one.

May Christ be with us!
May Christ be before us!
May Christ be in us,
Christ be over all!

May Thy Grace, Lord,
Always be ours,
This day, O Lord, and forevermore. Amen.

**SAINT PATRICK**

# DO

## WEEK 5, DAY 5

*Take some time today, by yourself or with others in your faith community, to carry out the following exercises, as you wrap your life around this week's truth.*

As we consider our Missionary Identity this week, today's "Day 5" follows the same pattern as the past two weeks. Here's the starting point, to jog your memory: as disciples of Christ we've each been given a new identity; as we consider our Missionary Identity this week, we must see that this gospel identity transcends whatever roles we play. But we don't get to ignore the fact that we're missionaries to God's world, committed to worship God through our obedience to his Great Commission. "Mission" isn't relegated to an event or different nation; it's within our everyday roles that we live out our renewed identities.

**1.** Today we consider how to live out our Missionary Identity, in the roles we play every day—because often our primary mission fields are the places we carry out many of these roles:

- Look back at the everyday roles you wrote in the chart on Weeks 3 and 4, "Day 5," and the position toward others in each role. If it would be helpful for you, rewrite those roles in the first column on the following chart, and in the second column rewrite your position toward others. And if you think of additional roles you haven't yet written, add them to Columns 1 and 2.

- In the third column, write some ways you can or do live out your Missionary Identity toward those you interact with in each role. (For example: building relationships during lunch hour, becoming a "regular" in neighborhood restaurants/pubs, etc.)

- In the fourth column, consider how often you've lived out your Missionary Identity well in that role. (1 = rarely; 2 = sometimes; 3 = more often than not; 4 = regularly)

- In the final column, for any you ranked yourself a "1" or "2," write some reasons it's difficult to live out your Missionary Identity within each role. Look back to Week One, Day Five and see if any of those reasons are excuses/idols.

| ROLE | POSITION | WAYS TO LIVE AS MISSIONARY | HOW OFTEN | WHY? |
|---|---|---|---|---|
| *Teacher* | *Authority to students; subordinate to dept. head* | *Lunch w/colleagues; engage with Jim's questions of identity; pray for students* | *2* | *Fear of boss; want to give a good impression; busyness* |
| | | | | |
| | | | | |
| | | | | |
| | | | | |

**2.** In your own words, explain the Missionary Identity. What does it mean that the gospel calls us into a servant relationship toward God and those he puts around us?

**3.** Write down some things you can do this week to display and speak the gospel to a few specific people in your community and your mission field. Then get practical: pray for God to lead and guide you, and practice obedience to his great commission!

## WEEK 5, DAY 6

Start by having someone share their story. The goal in sharing stories is to listen for things to celebrate and thank God for, and to listen for themes or areas of life to ask questions and speak truth in love, as you point each other toward Jesus. After they share, pray for the person who shared and ask who will share next week.

*Based on this week's reading, questions, prayers, and activities, honestly discuss questions like the following with your faith community. The tendency is going to want to stay general: get gritty and specific. Commit to putting your belief into action, by planning one or two specific ways to carry out each. Lovingly speak truth into areas of weakness, and figure out together how to encourage each other to infuse the gospel into this week's regular rhythms. And remember, some of this – maybe most of this – can't be limited to the one "official" meeting of your community each week, and this discussion is simply acknowledging who you are personally, as a redeemed follower of Jesus, as you do life together.*

1. From this week's personal preparation, what stood out to you? What was new? What was exciting/hopeful?

2. From this week's personal preparation, is there anything you're confused by/have questions about? What was difficult to read/ponder?

3. As disciples of Jesus, how does the gospel call us to be missionaries? Why is this a vital element of living out our faith in the everyday stuff of life?

4. As a community, are there ways we can celebrate God's work in helping us live out this identity well? (For example: how well do we go into the darkness and rearrange our lives around our mission field[s], do we often rely on God the Spirit to lead us, is God producing fruit for his kingdom, through our humble obedience?)

5. Using those same criteria, can we celebrate ways God's led our community to live out our Missionary Identity in and toward those in our mission field?

6. Are there areas we need to grow together, in living out this identity? As we worked through this week's content, what are some ways we came up with, by which we might help each other live as missionaries better than we are?

7. Does anyone need help with the things you wrote down on Day 5, knowing how to live out this identity in a certain role, or coming up with missionary efforts we can carry out together? What do you need from our community to help carry these out, and/or how can we encourage each other to do them well?

8. Is there anything we've discussed tonight that anyone wants to commit to follow-up on or do together in the coming week or beyond? Why or why not?

⊙ *Close your meeting in prayer.*

# REST

## WEEK 5, DAY 7

Knowing we're all busy, and that we all get behind, one day each week doesn't have specific assignments. It's simply a "floating day off" to encourage you to rest and dwell on this week's theme. This day to rest and recreate is designed to break up your week, and to remind you of God's truth and promises: He is sufficient for our every need, we rely on His power and leading to accomplish anything good, we don't have to work to earn his approval, and He is in control regardless of our action or inaction.

WEEK 6

THE EVERYDAY STUFF

# Rhythms, part 1

# START

## WEEK 6, DAY 1

For video and additional resources pertaining to Week 6, visit:

www.saturatetheworld.com/fg/week6

*Prayerfully and thoughtfully read this week's reading (or read chapters 15 and 17 of* Saturate*). As you read, circle, underline, write in the margins, and interact with concepts or ideas that are new, difficult, inspiring, etc.*

Living out the family, missionary, and servant identities we've discussed should not be—and cannot be—relegated to mere activities we do, on top of everything else that fills our lives. That's not how God designed life to work! If we're learning to see all of life through the lens of the gospel, how do we wrap our lives around the gospel and our identities? In other words, "How do we infuse the gospel into the everyday stuff of life?"

### EVERYDAY RHYTHMS

Seeing church mainly as an event creates a significant problem for mission, because most people are very busy. And the more we fill our lives with church events and programs, the more we get pulled out of everyday life with people who don't yet know Jesus. Besides, we will never be able to live out our identities as family, servants, and missionaries in one or two church events a week. It must involve everyday life. We need to see that life is the program, because people need to see what it means to follow Jesus in the everyday stuff of life.

We realized we needed to help our people see that life has a normal rhythm. All people everywhere are engaged in things that happen in rhythm—day in and day out. When we engage in these everyday rhythms with Jesus-centered, Spirit-led direction, mission can happen any time and everywhere, and anybody can be a part of it.

If we're not going to add things to our busy lives, then the question we ask this week and next is, "How do we infuse the gospel into the everyday stuff of life?" The answer comes in understanding our everyday rhythms.

We'll look at three of the rhythms—eat, celebrate, and recreate—this week. Next week we'll consider three more—listen, story, and bless. But the idea of these two weeks is that since everyone does these six things, they're some of the best, easiest ways to live out the gospel and infuse our gospel identities into our everyday lives—we just have to be intentional about doing so.

## EAT

"Eating" means we regularly eat meals with others, as a display of the love, provision, and acceptance of God. We overcome idols like selfishness (giving up "family time" and extra cost to feed others), perfection ("the house is a mess"), safety ("they're not like me"), and control (when folks just show up). We "lay down our lives" and invite people in – followers of Jesus or not – and generously share good food and drink with them.

Something very significant happens at a meal. We are hungry. We are in need. And that need is met only by something outside of our bodies. It's interesting that Jesus called himself "the bread of life" (John 6:35). We have a deep spiritual hunger that can be met only by Jesus ... When people eat together, they experience something more than a physical event. A spiritual event takes place, whether they acknowledge it or not. God has provided a means to sustain life outside of our own lives, and whenever we eat, we are experiencing God's care and provision.

The meal creates an experience of unity—of oneness at a table. This is why most business deals take place during meals and why more conversation happens when people have drinks in their hands or are sitting together around a table. This is also why Jesus was called a friend of sinners—he identified with them over meals (Matt. 11:19). And this is why the Lord's Supper or Eucharist is also called Communion—it is a common meal eaten together to remind us of a common provision we share. We are one in our need and one in taking in God's provision for our need—thus, we have communion.

You're already eating, probably three times a day. Don't do it alone. Do it with others and watch Jesus join you at the table and change the meal. He's well acquainted with joining people at the table. Invite him to dinner with a few others and see what he does.

## CELEBRATE

"Celebration" means that when we gather together, God is the reason we celebrate. Celebrations, festivals, and parties are seen throughout the Bible and history. By seeing God as the reason to celebrate everything, this rhythm asks you to think about what you celebrate, and to create times to remember and display the One who is truly worth celebrating.

Everybody engages in some form of celebration, from birthday parties to national holidays. Disciples celebrate the grace of God given to us through Jesus in order to express how good and gracious God is. As people made in the image of God, we were created to celebrate. God celebrates. He parties! When God created, he celebrated. He said, "This is very good!" God's Word also directs us to celebrate his good work with him.

God's people look back to what God has done for us through Jesus and forward to what we will enjoy forever in Jesus's presence. We celebrate these blessings. Jesus actually compared his kingdom to a great party (Matthew 22:1-2). One day, we will have an amazing celebration, with Jesus at the center of the party (Revelation 19:6-9). [In bringing the better wine to the party at Cana (John 2:1-11), Jesus was bringing what they lacked in a generous and loving way. In stripping down to take on the posture of a servant sent to wash his disciples' feet (John 13:1-11), Jesus was bringing a servant towel for clean-up. And in the lives of those around us, sometimes there is simply no party where there should be one. As disciples of Jesus, we follow Jesus by bringing] what is lacking to the celebrations in our culture.

Let's host parties for friends' birthdays, anniversaries, or accomplishments—and as we do, let's celebrate God's work in and through them (whether they follow Jesus or not!). Let's enjoy holidays—and as we do, let's (for example) give thanks to the Giver of everything in November, celebrate eternal freedom in July, and outright party at Easter. Let's give good gifts; let's 'bring the better wine' (literally and figuratively)! The kingdom is like a party. And we are the party people, because we belong to the King who parties. He is the best at celebrating.

## RECREATE

"ReCreate" is our word for the rhythm of "rest and create." "ReCreating" means we take time to rest, play, create, and restore beauty, in ways that reflect God to ourselves and to others.

Our God created and then rested. He didn't stop sustaining the universe and take a nap. His rest was a deep satisfaction with what he had created. His creation was very good. If you believe the good news of Jesus Christ, you also are able to truly rest. We can live with the confidence that God is running the world, so we don't have to. We can be settled at heart, knowing that Jesus has done all the work necessary to make us acceptable to God, so we no longer need to try to earn his acceptance through our work. We can work with all of our hearts unto the Lord out of gratitude, and actually be at rest while we are working.

And if we believe the gospel, we can create amazing stuff as an outpouring of our new identity as new-creation people. In fact, those of us who are in Christ should be the most creative people, because we have been freed from enslavement to the approval of others, and we also are daily becoming more like our Creator. Because he has restored and is restoring us, we also are able to bring restoration to things broken, distorted, or marred by sin. This leads us to work in a state of rest, create at rest, and play at rest.

I have discovered that my lack of faith in God's power to save, sustain, and secure me is displayed in my lack of ability to truly rest, create, and play ... Too many of us can't rest and create. But we should be the most playfully rested people on Earth, because our Dad has it all taken care of for us!

## DAY 1: QUESTIONS TO CONSIDER

1. When, where, and with whom do you normally eat? What is the typical tone of your breakfasts, your lunches, and your dinners? (For example: rushed, relaxed, tense, celebratory)

2. What holidays, events, and everyday things do you typically celebrate? Considering the past year, what has each of those celebrations looked like?

3. In a typical month, how well and how often do you rest and have fun? What types of things do you do when you rest and play?

4. Do you consider yourself a creative person? If you don't, was there a time in your life when you did, and what would you create if you could? If you do, what types of things do you create?

# READ

## WEEK 6, DAY 2

*Prayerfully and thoughtfully read the biblical texts below, then spend a few moments reflecting on the truths therein by answering the questions at the end.*

Where do you see this week's three rhythms in the following verses, whether explicitly mentioned, implied by actions, or as simply necessary to rightly understand the passage?

◘ Box areas you see "eating" through a gospel lens

○ Circle areas you see "celebrating" well

★ Star areas you see "recreating" (resting, playing, creating, and restoring) well

### GENESIS 1:1-2:3

In the beginning, God created the heavens and the earth. The earth was without form and void, and darkness was over the face of the deep. And the Spirit of God was hovering over the face of the waters.

And God said, "Let there be light," and there was light. And God saw that the light was good. And God separated the light from the darkness. God called the light Day, and the darkness he called Night. And there was evening and there was morning, the first day. And God said, "Let there be an expanse in the midst of the waters, and let it separate the waters from the waters." And God made the expanse and separated the waters that were under the expanse from the waters that were above the expanse. And it was so. And God called the expanse Heaven. And there was evening and there was morning, the second day. And God said, "Let the waters under the heavens be gathered together into one place, and let the dry land appear." And it was so. God called the dry land Earth, and the waters that were gathered together he called Seas. And God saw that it was good. And God said, "Let the earth sprout vegetation, plants yielding seed, and fruit trees bearing fruit in which is their seed, each according to its kind, on the earth." And it was so. The earth brought forth vegetation, plants yielding seed according to their own kinds, and trees bearing fruit in which is their seed, each according to its kind. And God saw that it was good. And there was evening and there was morning, the third day.

And God said, "Let there be lights in the expanse of the heavens to separate the day from the night. And let them be for signs and for seasons, and for days and years, and let them be lights in the expanse of the heavens to give light upon the earth." And it was so. And God made the two great lights—the greater light to rule the day and the lesser light to rule the night—and the stars. And God set them in the expanse of the heavens to give light on he earth, to rule over the day and over the night, and to separate the light from the darkness. And God saw that t was good. And there was evening and there was morning, the fourth day. And God said, "Let the waters swarm with swarms of living creatures, and let birds fly above the earth across the expanse of the heavens." So God created the great sea creatures and every living creature that moves, with which the waters swarm, according to their kinds, and every winged bird according to its kind. And God saw that it was good. And God blessed them, saying, "Be fruitful and multiply and fill the waters in the seas, and let birds multiply on the earth." And there was evening and there was morning, the fifth day. And God said, "Let the earth bring forth living creatures according to their kinds—livestock and creeping things and beasts of the earth according to their kinds." And it was so. And God made the beasts of the earth according to their kinds and the livestock according to their kinds, and everything that creeps on the ground according to its kind. And God saw that it was good.

Then God said, "Let us make man in our image, after our likeness. And let them have dominion over the fish of the sea and over the birds of the heavens and over the livestock and over all the earth and over every creeping thing that creeps on the earth."

So God created man in his own image,
in the image of God he created him;
male and female he created them.

And God blessed them. And God said to them, "Be fruitful and multiply and fill the earth and subdue it, and have dominion over the fish of the sea and over the birds of the heavens and over every living thing that moves on the earth." And God said, "Behold, I have given you every plant yielding seed that is on the face of all the earth, and every tree with seed in its fruit. You shall have them for food. And to every beast of the earth and to every bird of the heavens and to everything that creeps on the earth, everything that has the breath of life, I have given every green plant for food." And it was so. And God saw everything that he had made, and behold, it was very good. And there was evening and there was morning, the sixth day.

Thus the heavens and the earth were finished, and all the host of them. And on the seventh day God finished his work that he had done, and he rested on the seventh day from all his work that he had done. So God blessed the seventh day and made it holy, because on it God rested from all his work that he had done in creation...

**MARK 2:27-28**

And he said to them, "The Sabbath was made for man, not man for the Sabbath. So the Son of Man is lord even of the Sabbath."

**LUKE 7:33 - 35**

For John the Baptist has come eating no bread and drinking no wine, and you say, 'He has a demon.' The Son of Man has come eating and drinking, and you say, 'Look at him! A glutton and a drunkard, a friend of tax collectors and sinners!' Yet wisdom is justified by all her children.

**JOHN 12:12-13**

The next day the large crowd that had come to the feast heard that Jesus was coming to Jerusalem. So they took branches of palm trees and went out to meet him, crying out, "Hosanna! Blessed is he who comes in the name of the Lord, even the King of Israel!"

**FOR MORE:**

Leviticus 23 / John 6:31-35 / 1 Corinthians 11:17-26

## DAY 2: QUESTIONS TO CONSIDER

Answer these questions as you think about what you saw in today's verses:

1. What themes jumped out to you as you examined the everyday rhythms of God and his people celebrating, resting, and creating, and of God's people eating?

**2.** What was the posture of God's people toward God as they carried out these three rhythms?

**3.** How is God's gospel displayed as his people eat, celebrate, and recreate?

There are plenty of stories, verses, and instances in the Bible where God's people didn't live out these rhythms to their intended purpose and glory of God. Think about what you know of the Bible and Story of God and answer the following questions. If you need a jumpstart, consider these passages: Genesis 3; Exodus 32; Isaiah 1; Romans 1:18-25; Acts 19:23-41; 1 Corinthians 11:17-34.

**4.** What are examples of God's people not eating well: where do they ignore God, or forget the meaning and symbolism found in general meals or in communion?

**5.** What are examples of God's people not celebrating well: where do they ignore what God has done for them, or celebrate "gods" other than God?

**6.** What are examples of God's people not recreating well: where do they overwork, seek their justification by their work, or cease to be creative or to work toward redeeming brokenness in the world?

# THINK

## WEEK 6, DAY 3

*Knowing that each week builds on previous weeks, prayerfully and honestly work through these questions and exercises, in light of previous weeks' and this week's themes.*

Consider how this week's three rhythms play out in your mind and life, by asking yourself the following questions about each rhythm. Don't feel like you need to answer every question: instead, choose those that most resonate with you, that you feel God the Spirit speaking to you through, or maybe those that are most challenging to you—either way, we encourage you to answer at least one question from each rhythm, and to write down your answers.

### DAY 3: QUESTIONS TO CONSIDER

#### THE RHYTHM OF EATING

**1.** In what ways might you view meals differently if you realized that every one is a way to remember and display the gospel?

**2.** How often do you share a meal with people in your faith community? How often do you share a meal with those who don't believe in the same things as you? Why?

### THE RHYTHM OF CELEBRATING

**3.** What are some of the things you celebrate more than you celebrate God? What do those things say about your identity?

**4.** What are some of the typical things you and your faith community celebrate? What are some of the typical things your mission field celebrates?

### THE RHYTHM OF RECREATING

**5.** What are some untruths, or false identities, that you believe that keep you from resting? What do those untruths or false identities promise about rest but don't deliver well? (example: "I feel like I have to be constantly checking in with work, even on weekends, because I worry that if something falls though the crack, it'll impact my boss's view of me and potentially my job. It becomes a control issue and makes me feel like the weight of the world is on my shoulders—I trust myself instead of God and others.")

6. What do you need to do to intentionally carve a rhythm of rest into your daily, weekly, monthly, and yearly schedule? What do you need to do to plan it, and what do you need to do to ensure that it happens?

---

FOR EXTRA STUDY

7. Which of these rhythms do you think you'd have the easiest time living out with intentionality? Which do you think would be the hardest for you? Why?

8. How do these three rhythms overlap and feed each other? (For example: eating is a great way to celebrate, and to bring others into your celebration.)

9. What questions or ideas do you have from this week's study that you want to discuss when you meet with your faith community?

# PRAY

## WEEK 6, DAY 4

Knowing that we're dependent on God to produce any good fruit in us, spend today walking through the following prayer exercises related to this week's theme.

### PRAYING THE PSALMS

The Psalms teach us how to approach God in raw, humble ways, and help us remember the truth of who God objectively is, despite our subjective discomfort or circumstances. Slowly consider the words of the psalm, trying to understand it, lingering over it. Then pray it several times as it is written or in your own words as a prayer to God.

#### PSALM 16

Preserve me, O God, for in you I take refuge.
I say to the LORD, "You are my Lord;
I have no good apart from you."

As for the saints in the land, they are the excellent ones,
in whom is all my delight.

The sorrows of those who run after another god
shall multiply;
their drink offerings of blood I will not pour out
or take their names on my lips.

The LORD is my chosen portion and my cup;
you hold my lot.
The lines have fallen for me in pleasant places;
indeed, I have a beautiful inheritance.

I bless the LORD who gives me counsel;
in the night also my heart instructs me.
I have set the LORD always before me;
because he is at my right hand, I shall not
be shaken.

Therefore my heart is glad, and my whole being rejoices;
my flesh also dwells secure.
For you will not abandon my soul to Sheol,
or let your holy one see corruption.

You make known to me the path of life;
in your presence there is fullness of joy;
at your right hand are pleasures forevermore.

## PSALM 145

I will extol you, my God and King,
    and bless your name forever and ever.
Every day I will bless you
    and praise your name forever and ever.
Great is the LORD, and greatly to be praised,
    and his greatness is unsearchable.

One generation shall commend your works to another,
    and shall declare your mighty acts.
On the glorious splendor of your majesty,
    and on your wondrous works, I will meditate.
They shall speak of the might of your awesome deeds,
    and I will declare your greatness.
They shall pour forth the fame of your abundant goodness
    and shall sing aloud of your righteousness.

The LORD is gracious and merciful,
    slow to anger and abounding in steadfast love.
The LORD is good to all,
    and his mercy is over all that he has made.

All your works shall give thanks to you, O LORD,
    and all your saints shall bless you!
They shall speak of the glory of your kingdom
    and tell of your power,
to make known to the children of man your mighty deeds,
    and the glorious splendor of your kingdom.
Your kingdom is an everlasting kingdom,
    and your dominion endures throughout all generations.

[The LORD is faithful in all his words
    and kind in all his works.]
The LORD upholds all who are falling
    and raises up all who are bowed down.
The eyes of all look to you,
    and you give them their food in due season.
You open your hand;
    you satisfy the desire of every living thing.
The LORD is righteous in all his ways
    and kind in all his works.
The LORD is near to all who call on him,
    to all who call on him in truth.
He fulfills the desire of those who fear him;
    he also hears their cry and saves them.
The LORD preserves all who love him,
    but all the wicked he will destroy.

My mouth will speak the praise of the LORD,
    and let all flesh bless his holy name forever and ever.

## CRAFT YOUR OWN PRAYER

In your own words, spend some intentional time talking to and listening for God along this week's theme. We encourage you to write your prayer, as well as thoughts that come to mind that God might be prompting. Test those thoughts against the truth of Scripture, as well as your community. Here are some things you might pray:

- Praise God for being worthy of celebration, for both providing and enabling worship through food and drink, and for his sovereign goodness, which allows us to rest.
- Thank God for specific areas of celebration, thank him for opportunities he's provided to live out your discipleship in specific ways around the table, and thank him for specific ways he's given you rest in the past season.
- Confess to God areas of sin, disbelief, or discomfort: maybe you feel it in the way you eat, the recipient of your celebrations, or your lack of rest; maybe it's in a lack of intentionality regarding these rhythms; maybe you're resting in a false identity which leads you to reject these rhythms.
- Look back at your answers to yesterday's questions. As you do, consider what jumps out to you, and ask God to lead you in his ways and truth, to help you see lies or untruths that you're believing about him or yourself, to remind you of his identity and work in and through you, and to redeem or restore any brokenness in those areas.
- Stop to listen, be still and quiet before God, and write down any thoughts that come to mind.

## HISTORIC PRAYER

In closing today's prayer exercises, ponder and pray the prayer below, which is pulled from historic Christian literature, and has been prayed by Jesus's disciples for many, many years.

> Our Father in heaven,
> hallowed be your name.
> Your kingdom come,
> your will be done,
> on earth as it is in heaven.
> Give us this day our daily bread,
> and forgive us our debts,
> as we also have forgiven our debtors.
> And lead us not into temptation,
> but deliver us from evil.
>
> JESUS OF NAZARETH, MATTHEW 6:9-13

# DO

## WEEK 6, DAY 5

*Take some time today, by yourself or with others in your faith community, to carry out the following exercises, as you wrap your life around this week's truth.*

The entire principle of everyday rhythm involves prayerfully considering things you already do, and infusing the gospel, and our new identity, into those things. With that in mind, read back over Day 1 of this week if you need to. Then, starting with your answers to this week's questions so far, get creative: think through how each rhythm currently looks in your life, and brainstorm how you can intentionally bring the gospel into what you already do, rather than adding something to your life.

| EAT | |
|---|---|
| 1. *List the different groups of people in your life who you spend time with.* | 2. *If your primary identity is a disciple of God, how might you prayerfully prioritize those different groups of people, as far as intentionally giving time to them?* |
| 3. *Consider the meals you eat each week: how can you prayerfully plan toward better balance of sharing meals with those groups? (For example, which meals should you block off for you/your family? How many should you open to your faith community or mission?)* | 4. *Get practical: list at least one person in your community, and at least one person in your mission field with whom you'll eat in the next week—then go set the meal(s) up!* |

| CELEBRATE | |
|---|---|
| 1. *If you don't celebrate well, why not? What do you think you disbelieve about God that hinders you from living out the greatest reason to celebrate?* | 2. *What are specific ways you can see upcoming celebrations as a means of remembering and displaying the gospel to your community and mission field?* |
| 3. *What does the culture around you celebrate? How can you join already-existing cultural celebrations in a way that both remembers and displays the gospel to your community and mission field?* | 4. *Get practical: what's the next celebration you'll set up? When will it be and with whom will you plan it? Then go start planning!* |

NOTES

| RECREATE | |
|---|---|
| 1. *List the different things God has uniquely wired you to enjoy as you rest, play, create, and restore.* | 2. *List all the different things in your life that would be defined as "work" (essentially anything that takes responsibility). Which take more time than they should, which would you give up if you could, and which "give you life and enjoyment"? Why?* |
| 3. *If your current weekly or monthly rhythms seem to lack fun, creative, and/or restful activities, list a few new activities you'd like to try. How might each help you rest in and enjoy God?* | 4. *Get practical: Pull out your calendar and think through the upcoming weeks: how can you intentionally guard the equivalent of one full day for "recreation"/ Sabbath each week? What will you do and why? Who all will be involved in that recreation?* |

NOTES

WEEK 6, DAY 6

Start by having someone share their story. The goal in sharing stories is to listen for things to celebrate and thank God for, and to listen for themes or areas of life to ask questions and speak truth in love, as you point each other toward Jesus. After they share, pray for the person who shared and ask who will share next week.

*Based on this week's reading, questions, prayers, and activities, honestly discuss questions like the following with your faith community. The tendency is going to want to stay general: get gritty and specific. Commit to putting your belief into action, by planning one or two specific ways to carry out each. Lovingly speak truth into areas of weakness, and figure out together how to encourage each other to infuse the gospel into this week's regular rhythms. And remember, some of this – maybe most of this – can't be limited to the one "official" meeting of your community each week, and this discussion is simply acknowledging who you are personally, as a redeemed follower of Jesus, as you do life together.*

1. From this week's personal preparation, what stood out to you? What was new? What was exciting/hopeful?

2. From this week's personal preparation, is there anything you're confused by/have questions about? What was difficult to read/ponder?

**3.** As a community, how well do we eat through a gospel lens? What can we do to share more meals/open our tables to each other better? To our mission field?

**4.** As a community, how well do we celebrate through a gospel lens? What are things we can do to remember and display God's goodness to each other and to our mission field?

**5.** As a community, how well do we recreate through a gospel lens? What are ways we can encourage each other to rest, play, create, and restore? How can we recreate better, to remember and display God's goodness to each other and to our mission field?

6. What are some of the ways you wrote down on Day 3 that these rhythms overlap and feed into each other?

7. What are some of the ideas we came up with in Day 5 in the third column of each rhythm? What do you need from our community to help carry these out, and/or how can we encourage each other to do them well?

8. Is there anything we've discussed tonight that anyone wants to commit to follow-up on or do together in the coming week or beyond? Why or why not?

⊙ *Close your meeting in prayer.*

# REST

## WEEK 6, DAY 7

Knowing we're all busy, and that we all get behind, one day each week doesn't have specific assignments. It's simply a "floating day off," to encourage you to rest and dwell on this week's theme. This day to rest and recreate is designed to break up your week, and to remind you of God's truth and promises: He is sufficient for our every need, we rely on His power and leading to accomplish anything good, we don't have to work to earn his approval, and He is in control regardless of our action or inaction.

WEEK 7

THE EVERYDAY STUFF

# Rhythms, part 2

# START

## WEEK 7, DAY 1

*Prayerfully and thoughtfully read this week's reading (or re-read chapters 15 and 17 of Saturate). As you read, circle, underline, write in the margins, and interact with concepts or ideas that are new, difficult, inspiring, etc.*

Last week we introduced to you six "gospel rhythms." To recap, all people everywhere are engaged in things that happen in rhythm—day in and day out. When we engage in these everyday rhythms with Jesus-centered, Spirit-led direction, mission can happen anytime and everywhere, and anybody can be a part of it.

### THREE MORE RHYTHMS

We worked through three rhythms—eat, celebrate, and recreate—last week. Now we turn to three more—listen, story, and bless. But the theme from last week remains: since everyone does these six things, they're some of the best, easiest ways to live out the gospel and infuse our identities into our everyday lives—we just have to be intentional about doing so.

### LISTEN

Everybody is listening all the time. But who or what are we listening to, and are we paying attention to what we're hearing? "Listening" means that we pay careful attention to God and others. By knowing God's story, setting aside time to listen to God's voice above others, and listening well to our family and mission field, we speak the greater truth of God's story and work to areas of disbelief – ours and "theirs," by comparing those other, lesser stories to Jesus's greater one.

We listen to God: As God's people, we have his Spirit in us, regularly speaking to us through the Scriptures as we read them and recall them; through his church as we interact with one another; and personally as we listen closely to his voice (in John 10:1-21, Jesus said his sheep hear and listen to his voice, and in John 14-15, he said his Spirit would be the means by which we abide with him and are led by him). Listening also reminds me that the Spirit can speak to others in our silence. In fact, our willingness to quiet our souls and care for others often creates the best space for the Spirit to work. One of Jesus's titles is "Wonderful Counselor" (Isa. 9:6). He said that when he left he would send "another Counselor" (John 14:16 RSV), the Holy Spirit, to come and dwell in us. If you are a child of God, you have the Counselor living in you.

We listen to others: People are interesting. If we will listen, we will discover this. They are image bearers of God. They are broken, marred, and not fully together, just like us—but they are image bearers nonetheless. It's amazing, when you take the time to listen, how much you can learn. You begin to see how amazingly unique and creative each one of God's image bearers is. One of the greatest gifts we can give one another is a set of open ears and a closed mouth. Sure, there are times to speak, but are we willing to listen to one another?

Quiet your soul and listen to God. And close your mouth once in a while and listen to others. Do both together, and you will find yourself joining in with the activity of the Spirit working through you as his dwelling place. Remember, you are the temple of the living God! If you will listen, people will find themselves meeting with God when they are with you, even though they are not fully aware of it. We have God to give to people. Why would we want to get in the way of that by talking the whole time we are with them?

## STORY

The idea of "story" means that we understand, experience, and intersect God's story and others' stories. As we learn to see all of life through the gospel lens, we live out our identities by knowing the story we're living, knowing others' stories and listening for "lesser stories," and finding ways to display God's better story, in our own lives, in our church family, and in our mission field.

Everybody lives in light of a larger story. They are rehearsing these stories in their minds all of the time, and the stories provide the lenses through which people view their worlds. A person's dominant story will significantly shape his beliefs, behaviors, and everything in his life.

We should all know God's story and regularly rehearse it to ourselves and to one other. We need to be regularly in God's Word, the Bible, in order to be acquainted with his story. We also need to listen well to others' stories so we are able to bring the good news of God's redemptive story to bear on the stories of those who don't yet know how God can redeem their brokenness.

## BLESS

To "bless" means we intentionally display God's grace through words, gifts, and actions. Followers of Jesus believe we've been blessed with unmerited favor and provision, and see our own blessings as a means God uses to bless others. We don't truly own anything, yet have more than we could have dreamed. So we use God's resources for God.

Everybody has been blessed. And God's people know they have been blessed to be a blessing. We give from what we have to others in the form of words, actions, or tangible gifts. Such blessing is not meant to be a once-in-a-while deal. God intends for us to live in a perpetual rhythm of blessing others. This truth is one of the distinctive aspects of God's people throughout God's story. Whatever God gives to his people, he plans to give through them to others who need what they have. We have been blessed to be a blessing.

Another way of saying all of this is: Live in such a

way that it would demand a "Jesus explanation." In other words, you wouldn't be able to explain what you do or why without needing to talk about Jesus. That's what this group had done. There was no way to explain their actions without also needing to talk about Jesus.

Ask the Spirit to show you who to bless and how to bless them. Listen, and then bless with words, actions, or gifts.

## AN INTEGRATED, INTENTIONAL LIFE

As a final point in this two-week conversation of rhythms, we must remember that as we see all of life through the lens of the gospel, everything becomes integrated: we don't make, say, just Monday your "Christian community" night, then Saturday morning our "mission time," and so on—that mindset puts on and takes off the various "hats" of each identity. But the truth of the gospel is that you're *always* a disciple of God: *every moment* we're part of the family of God, we're *always* servants, and we're *never NOT* missionaries.

The beauty of our daily lives is that God has designed each of us—and indeed, every human in every culture in all of history—with the ability for our gospel identities to intertwine in simple ways: our identities and rhythms overlap as we live out God's objective story. As just one example, it's as we listen well to stories that we know how to bless and what to celebrate, and it's common to hear those stories around a table or while playing together.

Bottom line: If you have the Spirit of Christ Jesus, you are part of his body, the church. Everything you do matters. You are never alone. He is always with you. And because of this, you are always showing people what being a disciple—one who knows and loves Jesus—is like. You are making disciples every moment. The real question is, "Who are you making disciples of?" Are you showing others what submission to Jesus in the normal stuff of life is like? Can they watch you, hang out with you, eat with you, and vacation with you, and see what it would be like if they were to love and obey Jesus in everyday life? Normal life is lived with gospel intentionality for the sake of seeing others come

---

## DAY 1: QUESTIONS TO CONSIDER

**1.** With what consistency do you listen to God? How do you normally listen to him? (For example: Bible reading? Prayer? Discerning the voice of the Spirit?)

2. How well would you say you listen to others? Does your listening stem more from a place of information gathering, compassion, genuine interest, looking to fix things, or something else?

3. Considering earlier weeks' conversations, what are some of the "lesser stories" you find yourself believing? How often do you remind yourself of the Story of God, to yourself or others?

4. In what tangible ways have you blessed others this past week? What was your motive in those blessings? If you can't think of ways you've blessed people, what can you do today?

# READ

## WEEK 7, DAY 2

*Prayerfully and thoughtfully read the biblical texts below, then spend a few moments reflecting on the truths therein by answering the questions at the end.*

Where do you see this week's three rhythms in the following verses, whether explicitly mentioned, implied by actions, or as simply necessary to rightly understand the passage?

◘ Box areas you see "listening" though a gospel lens

○ Circle areas you see "stories" being shared and celebrated well

★ Star areas you see "blessing" well

### GENESIS 12:1-3

Now the LORD said to Abram, "Go from your country and your kindred and your father's house to the land that I will show you. And I will make of you a great nation, and I will bless you and make your name great, so that you will be a blessing. I will bless those who bless you, and him who dishonors you I will curse, and in you all the families of the earth shall be blessed."

### LEVITICUS 19:9-10

"When you reap the harvest of your land, you shall not reap your field right up to its edge, neither shall you gather the gleanings after your harvest. And you shall not strip your vineyard bare, neither shall you gather the fallen grapes of your vineyard. You shall leave them for the poor and for the sojourner: I am the LORD your God.

### PSALM 145:4-7

One generation shall commend your works to another,<br>
 and shall declare your mighty acts.<br>
On the glorious splendor of your majesty,<br>
 and on your wondrous works, I will meditate.<br>
They shall speak of the might of your awesome deeds,<br>
 and I will declare your greatness.<br>
They shall pour forth the fame of your abundant goodness<br>
 and shall sing aloud of your righteousness.

### MARK 1:35

And rising very early in the morning, while it was still dark, [Jesus] departed and went out to a desolate place, and there he prayed.

### JOHN 16:13-14

When the Spirit of truth comes, he will guide you into all the truth, for he will not speak on his own authority, but whatever he hears he will speak, and he will declare to you the things that are to come. He will glorify me, for he will take what is mine and declare it to you.

### ACTS 2:42-47

And they devoted themselves to the apostles' teaching and the fellowship, to the breaking of bread and the prayers. And awe came upon every soul, and many wonders and signs were being done through the apostles. And all who believed were together and had all things in common. And they were selling their possessions and belongings and distributing the proceeds to all, as any had need. And day by day, attending the temple together and breaking bread in their homes, they received their food with glad and generous hearts, praising God and having favor with all the people. And the Lord added to their number day by day those who were being saved.

### HEBREWS 10:24-25

And let us consider how to stir up one another to love and good works, not neglecting to meet together, as is the habit of some, but encouraging one another, and all the more as you see the Day drawing near.

### EPHESIANS 1:3-4

Blessed be the God and Father of our Lord Jesus Christ, who has blessed us in Christ with every spiritual blessing in the heavenly places, even as he chose us in him before the foundation of the world, that we should be holy and blameless before him.

---

### FOR MORE:

Psalm 19 / Luke 24:25-27 / Romans 12:13 / 2 Timothy 3:16-17 / Hebrews 1:1-3

## DAY 2: QUESTIONS TO CONSIDER

Answer these questions as you think about what you saw in today's verses:

1. What themes jumped out to you as you examined the everyday rhythms of God and his people blessing, and God's people sharing stories and listening?

2. What was the posture of God's people toward God as they carried out these three rhythms?

3. How is God's gospel displayed as his people listen, share stories, and bless?

The verses above display areas where God's people lived out these rhythms well. But there are plenty of stories, verses, and instances in the Bible where God's people didn't. Think about what you know of the Bible and answer these questions. If you need a jumpstart, consider these passages: Genesis 3; Exodus 17; Nehemiah 9; Acts 5; Romans 16:17-20; Galatians 2:11-21.

**4.** What are examples of God's people not sharing stories well: where do they listen to or believe a "lesser" story, or ignore stories of others or their culture?

**5.** What are examples of God's people *not* listening well: where do they ignore God, or listen to other voices over God's?

**6.** What are examples of God's people *not* blessing well: where do they turn inward, act selfishly, and use their resources only for themselves, instead of for God and others?

# THINK

## WEEK 7, DAY 3

*Knowing that each week builds on previous weeks, prayerfully and honestly work through these questions and exercises, in light of previous weeks' and this week's themes.*

Consider how this week's three rhythms play out in your mind and life, by asking yourself the following questions in light of each rhythm. Don't feel like you need to answer every question: instead, choose those that most resonate with you, that you feel God the Spirit speaking to you through, or maybe those that are most challenging to you—either way, we encourage you to answer at least one question from each rhythm, and to write down your answers.

### DAY 3: QUESTIONS TO CONSIDER

#### THE RHYTHM OF SHARING STORIES

**1.** Do you know how to tell your own story, and to show how Jesus is the hero who redeemed your story? Whether you're a follower of Jesus or not, in what areas in your life are you still believing another story over God's?

**2.** How well do you know the stories of those in your faith community? How well do you know the story of your mission field? Where in their own stories do they need to know and believe God's greater story?

## THE RHYTHM OF LISTENING

**3.** Do you set aside intentional time to listen to God through his Word and by his Spirit, regarding both your own life and the lives of those around you?

**4.** How well do you listen to those in your community? How well do you listen to your mission field? As you've listened, what are beliefs/questions underneath the surface conversation?

## THE RHYTHM OF BLESSING

**5.** What are some of the ways you've been blessed? List some of the ways you've been able to use those blessings to bless others. Or write some reasons why you might commonly see some of the resources you've been given primarily as yours and for yourself.

6. What are some of the needs in your community and mission field? What are some tangible ways you can bless them?

## FOR EXTRA STUDY

7. Which of these rhythms do you think you'd have the easiest time living out with intentionality? Which do you think would be the hardest for you? Why?

8. How do these three rhythms, and last week's too, overlap and feed each other? (For example: as you learn peoples' stories and listen to God's leading, you know how to bless others in a way that leads to a specific gospel need in their lives.)

9. What questions or ideas do you have from this week's study that you want to discuss when you meet with your faith community?

# PRAY

## WEEK 7, DAY 4

*Knowing that we're dependent on God to produce any good fruit in us, spend today walking through the following prayer exercises related to this week's theme.*

## PRAYING THE PSALMS

The Psalms teach us how to approach God in raw, humble ways, and help us remember the truth of who God objectively is, despite our subjective discomfort or circumstances. Slowly consider the words of the psalm, trying to understand it, lingering over it. Then pray it several times as it is written or in your own words as a prayer to God.

**PSALM 85** *To the choirmaster. A Psalm of the Sons of Korah.*

LORD, you were favorable to your land;
you restored the fortunes of Jacob.
You forgave the iniquity of your people;
you covered all their sin. Selah
You withdrew all your wrath;
you turned from your hot anger.

Restore us again, O God of our salvation,
and put away your indignation toward us!
Will you be angry with us forever?
Will you prolong your anger to all generations?
Will you not revive us again,
that your people may rejoice in you?
Show us your steadfast love, O LORD,
and grant us your salvation.

Let me hear what God the LORD will speak,
for he will speak peace to his people, to his saints;
but let them not turn back to folly.
Surely his salvation is near to those who fear him,
that glory may dwell in our land.

Steadfast love and faithfulness meet;
righteousness and peace kiss each other.
Faithfulness springs up from the ground,
and righteousness looks down from the sky.
Yes, the LORD will give what is good,
and our land will yield its increase.
Righteousness will go before him
and make his footsteps a way.

**PSALM 44** *To the choirmaster. A Maskil of the Sons of Korah.*

O God, we have heard with our ears,
our fathers have told us,
what deeds you performed in their days,
in the days of old:
you with your own hand drove out the nations,
but them you planted;
you afflicted the peoples,
but them you set free;
for not by their own sword did they win the land,
nor did their own arm save them,
but your right hand and your arm,
and the light of your face,
for you delighted in them.

You are my King, O God;
ordain salvation for Jacob!
Through you we push down our foes;
through your name we tread down those who rise up against us.
For not in my bow do I trust,
nor can my sword save me.
But you have saved us from our foes
and have put to shame those who hate us.
In God we have boasted continually,
and we will give thanks to your name forever. *Selah*

But you have rejected us and disgraced us
and have not gone out with our armies.
You have made us turn back from the foe,
and those who hate us have gotten spoil.
You have made us like sheep for slaughter
and have scattered us among the nations.
You have sold your people for a trifle,
demanding no high price for them.
You have made us the taunt of our neighbors,
the derision and scorn of those around us.

You have made us a byword among the nations,
a laughingstock among the peoples.
All day long my disgrace is before me,
and shame has covered my face
at the sound of the taunter and reviler,
at the sight of the enemy and the avenger.

All this has come upon us,
though we have not forgotten you,
and we have not been false to your covenant.
Our heart has not turned back,
nor have our steps departed from your way;
yet you have broken us in the place of jackals
and covered us with the shadow of death.
If we had forgotten the name of our God
or spread out our hands to a foreign god,
would not God discover this?
For he knows the secrets of the heart.
Yet for your sake we are killed all the day long;
we are regarded as sheep to be slaughtered.

Awake! Why are you sleeping, O Lord?
Rouse yourself! Do not reject us forever!
Why do you hide your face?
Why do you forget our affliction and oppression?
For our soul is bowed down to the dust;
our belly clings to the ground.
Rise up; come to our help!
Redeem us for the sake of your steadfast love!

## CRAFT YOUR OWN PRAYER

In your own words, spend some intentional time talking to and listening for God along this week's theme. We encourage you to write your prayer, as well as thoughts that come to mind that God might be prompting. Test those thoughts against the truth of Scripture, as well as your community. Here are some things you might pray:

- Remind yourself of the story of God: Creation and Fall in Genesis 1-3, aspects of his redemption and grace through the Old Testament, the climax of redemption in the gospels, aspects of his redemption and grace through the New Testament, and his promise of restoration in Revelation.

- If you're a follower of Jesus, celebrate the way that God's story intertwines with yours, and specific ways his always proves to be better than yours: think of your salvation, as well as moments before and after it. Praise God for his blessings in every aspect of your story.

- Confess to God areas of sin, disbelief, or discomfort: maybe you don't listen to others, or haven't seen the resources he gives as the means by which he wants to bless others. Maybe you are relying on your own story, or any other "lesser" story than God's. Maybe it's in a lack of intentionality regarding these rhythms; maybe you're resting in a false identity which leads you to reject these rhythms.

- Look back at your answers to yesterday's questions. As you do, consider what jumps out to you, and ask God to lead you in his ways and truth, to help you see lies or untruths that you're believing about him or yourself, to remind you of his identity and work in and through you, and to redeem or restore any brokenness in those areas.

- Stop to listen, be still and quiet before God, and write down any thoughts that come to mind.

## HISTORIC PRAYER

In closing today's prayer exercises, ponder and pray the prayer below, which is pulled from historic Christian literature, and has been prayed by Jesus's disciples for many, many years.

> The radiance of the Father's splendor, the Father's visible image, Jesus Christ our God, peerless among counselors, Prince of Peace, Father of the world to come, the model after which Adam was formed, for our sakes became like a slave: in the womb of Mary the virgin, without assistance from any man, he took flesh.
>
> Enable us, Lord, to reach the end of this luminous feast in peace, forsaking all idle words, acting virtuously, shunning our passions, and raising ourselves above the things of this world.
>
> Bless your church, which you brought into being long ago and attached to yourself through your own life-giving blood. Help all orthodox pastors, heads of churches, and doctors [theologians].
>
> Bless your servants, whose trust is all in you; bless all Christian souls, the sick, those tormented by evil spirits, and those who have asked us to pray for them.
>
> Show yourself as merciful as you are rich in grace; save and preserve us; enable us to obtain those good things to come which will never know an end.
>
> May we celebrate your glorious birth, and the Father who sent you to redeem us, and your Spirit, the Giver of life, now and forever, age after age. Amen.

A SYRIAC CHRISTMAS LITURGY (LATE THIRD OR EARLY FOURTH CENTURY)

# DO

## WEEK 7, DAY 5

*Take some time today, by yourself or with others in your faith community, to carry out the following exercises, as you wrap your life around this week's truth.*

The entire principle of everyday rhythm involves prayerfully considering things you already do, and infusing the gospel, and our new identity, into those things. With that in mind, read back over Day 1 of this week if you need to. Then, starting with your answers to this week's questions so far, get creative: think through how each rhythm currently looks in your life, and brainstorm how you can intentionally bring the gospel into what you already do, rather than adding something to your life.

| LISTEN | |
|---|---|
| 1. *What moments in your day are you most intentionally listening, and to what/whom? (For example: news, your boss, reading before bed.)* | 2. *In what ways can you more intentionally listen to God in those moments and throughout each day, more than the other "voices"?* |
| 3. *In what ways can your faith community listen better to each other? How can you listen better to your mission field?* | 4. *Get practical: think of someone in your community and someone in your mission field whose stories you don't know. When and how will you carve out time to intentionally get to know their stories? Then go set it up!* |

| STORY | |
|---|---|
| 1. *When and with whom do you currently share stories? What are your stories about? What are their stories about?* | 2. *How can you bring God's gospel story into your own stories?* |
| 3. *How can you engage others' stories, and your mission field's stories well?* | 4. *Get practical: list someone in your community and someone in your mission field with whom you'll share at least part of God's story this week. When will you do that, why did you choose those people, and in what part of their own story do they need to hear God's?* |

NOTES

| BLESS | |
|---|---|
| *List as many resources as you can think of that God's given you. How does each uniquely remind you of God's goodness to you?* | 2. *Prayerfully list as many ways as you can think of that each resource could bless others in your faith community/mission field.* |
| . *List some current needs you have: would you courageously and humbly bring those needs to others in your community or mission field?* | 4. *Get practical: if you know of needs that others have, and God has given you resources to help meet those needs, get in touch with those people and bless them—even if it takes some sacrifice on your part. If you don't know others' needs, go ask!* |

NOTES

## WEEK 7, DAY 6

Start by having someone share their story. The goal in sharing stories is to listen for things to celebrate and thank God for, and to listen for themes or areas of life to ask questions and speak truth in love, as you point each other toward Jesus. After they share, pray for the person who shared and ask who will share next week.

*Based on this week's reading, questions, prayers, and activities, honestly discuss questions like the following with your faith community. The tendency is going to want to stay general: get gritty and specific. Commit to putting your belief into action, by planning one or two specific ways to carry out each. Lovingly speak truth into areas of weakness, and figure out together how to encourage each other to infuse the gospel into this week's regular rhythms. And remember, some of this – maybe most of this – can't be limited to the one "official" meeting of your community each week, and this discussion is simply acknowledging who you are personally, as a redeemed follower of Jesus, as you do life together.*

1. From this week's personal preparation, what stood out to you? What was new? What was exciting/hopeful?

2. From this week's personal preparation, is there anything you're confused by/have questions about? What was difficult to read/ponder?

3. How well does our community listen to God? What are ways we can listen to God better, through his word, by his Spirit, and on behalf of others?

4. How well do we listen to each other? To our mission fields? What are ways we can encourage each other to listen better?

5. As a community, how well do we share stories? What are ways we can know each other's stories better? How can we learn the stories of our mission fields?

**6.** In what ways do those in our community bless each other? From Day 5, are there any needs among us that need to be considered/met? How can we meet the needs of our mission fields?

**7.** What are some of the ideas we came up with in Day 5, of ways to live out each rhythm? How can our community join each other and/or encourage each other to do them well?

**8.** Is there anything we've discussed tonight that anyone wants to commit to follow-up on or do together in the coming week or beyond? Why or why not?

⊙ *Close your meeting in prayer.*

# REST

## WEEK 7, DAY 7

Knowing we're all busy, and that we all get behind, one day each week doesn't have specific assignments. It's simply a "floating day off," to encourage you to rest and dwell on this week's theme. This day to rest and recreate is designed to break up your week, and to remind you of God's truth and promises: He is sufficient for our every need, we rely on His power and leading to accomplish anything good, we don't have to work to earn his approval, and He is in control regardless of our action or inaction.

WEEK 8

THE EVERYDAY STUFF

# Commission

# START

## WEEK 8, DAY 1

*Prayerfully and thoughtfully read this week's reading (or read chapter16 and Conclusion of* Saturate*). As you read, circle, underline, write in the margins, and interact with concepts or ideas that are new, difficult, inspiring, etc.*

For video and additional resources pertaining to Week 8, visit:

www.saturatetheworld.com/fg/week8

This week is a little different than the rest of the Field Guide has been. Instead of introducing new content, we're going revisit the past seven weeks, compile the content into a picture of a life of holistic discipleship, and consider making a plan for pursuing this life of discipleship together. We can tend to forget who we are and what God has called us to do together.

### AN EVERYDAY PLAN

Over time, a missional community can subtly become primarily a support group that is only concerned about one another, forgetting the mission of making disciples of others. Some groups, especially if the members have been in the church for some time, gravitate toward only doing a Bible study together, so they need to be reoriented toward also obeying God's Word while on mission together. We've also observed that missional communities can turn into social-activist groups, with little or no gospel proclamation—good deeds with no words about Jesus—while others may become outwardly focused on mission while failing to commit to seeing one another develop into maturity. Yet another ongoing challenge is keeping groups from expecting to accomplish everything we've talked about in a couple of hours a week and a special event here or there.

So we encourage our groups to reform their missional community covenants every year. Missional communities establish these covenants when they form in order to shape how they will live out their identities and rhythms in particular mission fields (see Appendix B for a blank Missional Community Covenant Template and Appendix C for a sample covenant). When our groups reform their covenants, they generally spend several weeks doing so, using our definition of a missional community—a family of missionary servants sent as disciples who make disciples—as a guide. The process moves through several steps:

#### 1. START WITH THE GOSPEL

The first step is making sure we all still affirm our belief in the gospel of Jesus Christ. We don't want to ever assume this, so it is the first part of our covenant. In fact, we encourage our groups not only to affirm their individual and collective belief in the gospel, but also to develop a plan for rehearsing it together regularly. We want everyone to be fluent in the gospel, speaking it regularly to one another and to those who don't yet believe.

If you are part of a group, forming a group, or looking to reform a group, please make sure you build a strong gospel foundation and have a plan to help everyone become fluent in speaking the truths of Jesus into the everyday stuff of life.[7]

## 2. CLARIFY THE MISSION

Next, we clarify our mission. We remind one another that we are commanded by Jesus to make disciples of all people groups. So we ask: "What people and place do we believe God is collectively sending us to this year? Who do we hope to see become followers of Jesus Christ?"

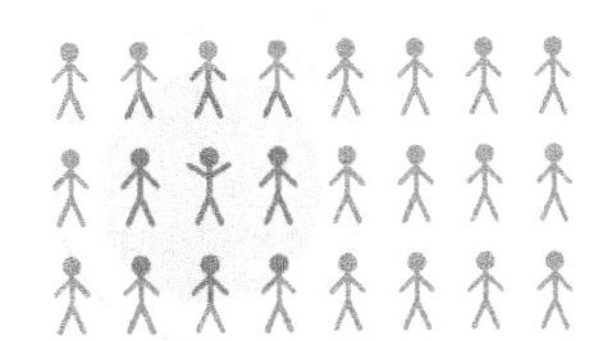

Whom do you believe God is sending you to? Who around you needs to know Jesus? Is there a neighborhood or network of relationships where people need to be loved like family, served as Jesus served you, and told about the good news of salvation found in Jesus's name? The possibilities for a missional focus are endless.

Some ask: "Why is having a missional focus so important? Isn't all of life mission? Isn't every one of us a missionary?" Yes, all of life is mission and everyone is a missionary. Life is the mission trip. However, we've found it's important to also identify a collective mission—a missional focus:

- Too often, groups primarily talk about being on mission, but then the members leave the group meeting and find themselves alone on mission. As a result, many don't engage in mission, or if they do, they are lonely missionaries.

- A missional focus also provides common experiences through which people can more effectively be trained. Another strength of a common missional focus is that the people we are sent to can see what Jesus saves us into—the family of God. We are not just saved from hell. We are saved for God's purposes now into life together on his mission.

- A missional focus also helps us with our individual missions, as it gives each of us a context into which to invite our friends, a context where they can also experience the gospel being worked out in community on mission.

7. For help with this, please visit **www.saturatetheworld.com/gospel-fluency**.

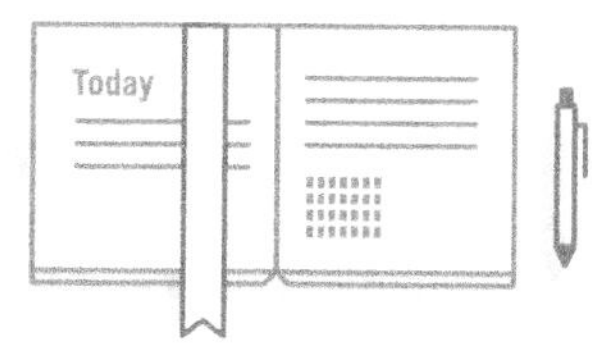


### 3. FORM A PLAN

Once we've clarified our mission, we walk through each of the identities, asking how we live in light of our identities in the everyday stuff of life. We then put the plan together and formally commit (some actually sign a document), with God's help, to faithfully fulfill it (note: we clarify that none of us will do this perfectly and that we all need the grace of the gospel to do it at all).

If you engage in this activity with a group, you will find it very difficult and hugely beneficial. It will be difficult because people will not immediately agree on everything. But they don't have to. In some cases, some in the group will want to commit to something, while others won't. That's fine, as people are in different places spiritually. The process will reveal levels of maturity and commitment, as well as fears, insecurities, selfishness, and pride. It will be beneficial because, if this process is led well, much discipleship of one another will take place. Issues and concerns will come up, revealing where people need to be reminded of the gospel and its implications. Remember, conflict is not bad. It provides a context for discipleship to happen.

## PERSONAL PREPARATION FOR A COLLECTIVE PLAN

Keep in mind that you may not want everyone in the group going through this process together. You may have a core that is very committed to the mission and eager to engage this process, while others don't really want to. Don't necessarily try to get everyone to walk through these steps right away. Some just aren't ready.

The rest of this week will guide you through the process of making a plan for living out this holistic vision for discipleship as you pursue obedience to God's call to Jesus saturation—in your household, neighborhood, workplace, school, city, nation, and world. Each day will walk through one aspect of a sample missional community plan: please prayerfully answer the questions, and since this is merely a template, add to or tweak the questions to fit your group and/or context. Days Two through Five this week prepare you for your group to come together and discuss your thoughts on Day Six.

Our deepest prayer is that the group you've been meeting with will commit to this plan together, and become a community of disciples seeking to make disciples, who live as family, servants, and missionaries together in the everyday stuff of life. If this specific group isn't going to—and there are both good and poor reasons for that decision!—this week's exercise will give you practice, and prepare you to find or start a group who will. And if nothing else, this week can serve as a foundation for your family and/or roommates, to be a seed in your neighborhood which may one day blossom into a flourishing vine, giving life and bearing fruit that's only found in Jesus.

# GOSPEL

## WEEK 8, DAY 2

*Prayerfully and thoughtfully work through today's section of the Missional Community Plan Template, reflecting on each statement and question below. If you need to, circle, underline, write in the margins, and interact with concepts or ideas that are new, difficult, inspiring, etc.*

### PREFACE

This template[8] serves as a guide for a committed group of Christians to form a plan together for being Jesus's disciples on mission. If you come back to it in coming years, you may want to preface the forming of this plan by working through the rest of this Field Guide first, or by doing a study on the gospel, your new identity in Christ, and the mission of making disciples. Or you could form your plan while doing a study on each of those important topics.

For today, we encourage you to thoughtfully read the following statements, affirming your belief in everything that Jesus is and does, in the past, present, and future aspects of his work. You might put a check mark next to each bullet point you wholeheartedly believe, a question mark next to bullet points you don't understand or question, and an X next to any bullet points you have a hard time believing or don't believe at all.

After reading all the belief statements, you'll find some questions at the end. We encourage you to ask any questions, and work through statements you marked with a "**?**" or "**X**" with someone in your community—either before or during Day Six's meeting.

### GOSPEL

I believe the gospel is the power of God for salvation through faith in the person and work of Jesus Christ saving me for the purpose of glorifying God and participating in his mission of saturation through making disciples who make disciples.

**I BELIEVE I HAVE BEEN SAVED FROM THE PENALTY OF SIN . . .**

- I believe I was an enemy of God because of my sin and rebellion against him, deserving his wrath.
- I believe Jesus is the Son of God who is fully God and fully man and that he lived his life fully submitted to God the Father.
- I believe Jesus died on the cross for my sins according to the Scriptures.

8. For a blank Missional Community Convenant Template, see Appendix B. For a sample of a completed covenant, see Appendix C.

- I believe Jesus rose again on the third day and appeared to many people.

- I believe Jesus ascended to the right hand of the Father and sent his Spirit to convict the world of sin, righteousness, and judgment.

- I believe the Holy Spirit has made me alive in Christ and I am now no longer condemned, but a new creation, loved by God as Father, submitted to Jesus as Lord, and sent and empowered by the Spirit for the mission of making disciples.

### I BELIEVE I AM BEING SAVED FROM THE POWER OF SIN . . .

- I believe that the Holy Spirit who raised Jesus from the dead now lives in me and I have access to the power of God to overcome sin and Satan today.

- I believe it is God's will that I be sanctified—set apart to do his will.

- I desire to obey God and continue to grow in becoming more like Jesus and accomplishing his mission.

- I believe I have all I need to make this a reality—his Spirit, his Word, and his church—and I intend to steward all of this for his glory.

### I BELIEVE I WILL BE SAVED FROM THE PRESENCE OF SIN . . .

- I believe Jesus will one day return and will make an end to sin, suffering, evil, and brokenness.

- I believe there will be a new heaven and a new earth.

- I believe he will judge the living and the dead, and all those who put their trust in Jesus's life, death, and resurrection on their behalf will enjoy being in God's presence forever in the new heaven and new earth.

- I believe all those who trust in something or someone other than Jesus for their life and justification before God will be separated from God forever.

- I believe it is our job as the church to proclaim the gospel of Jesus Christ for the salvation of souls and to display through our lives a foretaste of the future so that people will hunger for it and put their faith in Jesus Christ.

## PERSONAL REFLECTION

*Today's content stems from Week One of this Field Guide. If any of today's concepts are confusing or seem new, you might go back and revisit that week's content, or read chapters 1-6 of* Saturate.

1. Are there any of the bullet point "belief statements" above that you marked with a "**?**"or "**X**"? If so, why are those statements difficult for you to believe and/or accept as true?

2. If you've never before confessed belief in these elements of the gospel, please let others in your community know, so they can celebrate your belief with you!

# GOSPEL IDENTITY — FAMILY

*Prayerfully and thoughtfully work through today's section of the Missional Community Plan Template, reflecting on each statement and question below. If you need to, circle, underline, write in the margins, and interact with concepts or ideas that are new, difficult, inspiring, etc.*

## PREFACE

Since God has designed our discipleship of Jesus and the rhythms of our everyday lives to overlap as we live out our family, servant, and missionary identities, Days Three to Five of this week ask you to consider how you'd suggest that your missional community live out each identity.

It's important to note, however, that all three identities incorporate our gospel rhythms—as you'll see in the questions for each day. And it's even more important to realize that no plan for living out these identities should be considered independent of our discipleship; instead, each helps us plan certain elements of our discipleship. If we lose sight of this reality, then this plan can feel like a legalistic burden, rather than the tangible tool it's meant to be.

Today we consider the "family" side of life on life, life in community, and life on mission discipleship, as followers of Jesus committed to make disciples who make disciples. Choose at least five of the questions below: to answer those questions, prayerfully consider your community and mission field, write down your thoughts, and prepare to share your ideas when you meet on Day Six.

## MY IDEAS FOR LIVING OUT OUR FAMILY IDENTITY

**We are children of God who love one another as family. How will we express our love as brothers and sisters adopted by the Father?**

**1.** How will we commit to listening prayer for one another?

2. What study or training do we need to go through as a group in light of where we all need to grow (keeping in mind personal discipleship goals)?

3. What actions will we commit to in order to express our love for one another as brothers and sisters? (Think of the "one-another" passages. There are around fifty New Testament passages containing the words "one another. Each one addresses how Christians ought to treat one another.)

4. Are any of us who believe the gospel not yet baptized? What next steps should we take in obeying Jesus's command to be baptized (Matthew 28:19-20)?

**5.** How will we honor the leaders in the larger church family appointed to shepherd us?

**6.** How will we make sure all of us know one another's stories?

**7.** How will we celebrate Communion together?

**8.** What meals will we share with one another, and how often?

**9.** In what ways will we intentionally celebrate together, and around what?

**10.** What regular rhythms of recreating will we commit to together?

## PERSONAL REFLECTION

*Today's content stems from Week Three of this Field Guide (with plenty of overlap with weeks Two, Six, and Seven). If any of today's concepts are confusing or seem new, you might go back and revisit that week's content, or read chapters 7-12 and 15 of* Saturate.

1. Do you have a hard time with any of the questions above? If so, why? Think back to Week One, Day Five—do any of those difficulties stem from areas of idolatry or disbelief? We encourage you to take your concerns to someone in your community, before you meet later this week.

2. Since today's questions are only a template, are there other things you'd add to this list? Anything you'd change? If so, list them here, and prepare to discuss with your community later this week.

# GOSPEL IDENTITY — SERVANT

## WEEK 8, DAY 4

*Prayerfully and thoughtfully work through today's section of the Missional Community Plan Template, reflecting on each statement and question below. If you need to, circle, underline, write in the margins, and interact with concepts or ideas that are new, difficult, inspiring, etc.*

### PREFACE

Today we consider the "servant" side of discipleship, as followers of Jesus committed to make disciples who make disciples, and how our community can live as servants in our everyday rhythms. Choose at least five of the questions below: to answer those questions, prayerfully consider your community and mission field, write down your thoughts, and prepare to share your ideas when you meet on Day Six.

### MY IDEAS FOR LIVING OUT OUR SERVANT IDENTITY

**We are servants of King Jesus committed to serving others. How will we tangibly demonstrate the impact of the gospel in service to King Jesus?**

1. What would good news look like to the people group we are sent to?

2. What needs the good news of Jesus in your context? In other words, where can you restore what is broken (whether physically, spiritually, or otherwise) through our words and actions?

3. How might we demonstrate Jesus's rule and reign through tangible service to those God is sending us to?

4. What specific projects or events do we need to accomplish or get involved in to demonstrate the restorative work of the kingdom of God?

5. How will we serve the disconnected or under-resourced among the people we are sent to?

6. How can we encourage one another to see our vocations and jobs as worship to our King?

7. How could we serve together during our weekly celebrations with the larger body?

8. How will we walk through Spirit-led giving to the church and others?

9. How can we commit to help one another grow in serving in light of each person's unique design by God (For example: identify spiritual gifts or personality types; write out personal mission statements)?

10. How will we intentionally share what we have with one another and those in need?

## PERSONAL REFLECTION

*Today's content stems from Week Four of this Field Guide (with plenty of overlap with weeks Two, Six, and Seven). If any of today's concepts are confusing or seem new, you might go back and revisit that week's content, or read chapters 7-11, 13, and 15 of* Saturate.

1. Do you have a hard time with any of the questions above? If so, why? Think back to Week One, Day Five—do any of those difficulties stem from areas of idolatry or disbelief? We encourage you to take your concerns to someone in your community, before you meet later this week.

2. Since today's questions are only a template, are there other things you'd add to this list? Anything you'd change? If so, list them here, and prepare to discuss with your community later this week.

# GOSPEL IDENTITY — MISSIONARY

## WEEK 8, DAY 5

*Prayerfully and thoughtfully work through today's section of the Missional Community Plan Template, reflecting on each statement and question below. If you need to, circle, underline, write in the margins, and interact with concepts or ideas that are new, difficult, inspiring, etc.*

### PREFACE

Today we consider the "missionary" side of discipleship, as followers of Jesus committed to make disciples who make disciples, and how our community can live as missionaries in our everyday rhythms. Choose at least five of the questions below: to answer those questions, prayerfully consider your community and mission field, write down your thoughts, and prepare to share your ideas when you meet on Day Six.

### MY IDEAS FOR LIVING OUT OUR MISSIONARY IDENTITY

**We are Holy Spirit-filled missionaries sent as disciples to make disciples. How will we commit ourselves as disciples who make disciples in the power of the Spirit?**

1. Which people group(s) will be our missional focus?

2. Are there places in your community where you could regularly hang out in order to build relationships with those we want to reach? For example, moving a family meal from someone's home to a restaurant. Going out for coffee. Or playing catch at a park instead of your back yard.

3. How will we invite others to join us at the table? How often will we try to eat with others we are trying to reach?

4. How will we commit to listening prayer for those God is sending us to?

5. What specifically will we do so that the people to whom we are sent will hear the gospel this year (For example: go through the *Story of God*, share our story with them, engage in a study)?

6. How will we engage in celebrating with the people group God is sending us to?

**7.** What celebrations are missing, where can we bring the better wine, or where can we bring the servant towel to the party?

**8.** How will we bless those we are being sent to in word or deed?

**9.** How will we play and rest with those God is sending us to?

**10.** What steps should each of us take this year to grow as disciples who make disciples (help each person identify at least two to three goals)?

## PERSONAL REFLECTION

*Today's content stems from Week Five of this Field Guide (with plenty of overlap with weeks Two, Six, and Seven). If any of today's concepts are confusing or seem new, you might go back and revisit that week's content, or read chapters 7-11, 14, and 15 of* Saturate.

1. Do you have a hard time with any of the questions above? If so, why? Think back to Week One, Day Five—do any of those difficulties stem from areas of idolatry or disbelief? We encourage you to take your concerns to someone in your community, before you meet later this week.

2. Since today's questions are only a template, are there other things you'd add to this list? Anything you'd change? If so, list them here, and prepare to discuss with your community later this week.

## WEEK 8, DAY 6

Start by having someone share their story. The goal in sharing stories is to listen for things to celebrate and thank God for, and to listen for themes or areas of life to ask questions and speak truth in love, as you point each other toward Jesus. After they share, pray for the person who shared.

*Based on this week's reading, questions, prayers, and activities, honestly discuss questions like the following with your faith community. The tendency is going to want to stay general: get gritty and specific. Commit to putting your belief into action, by planning one or two specific ways to carry out each. Lovingly speak truth into areas of weakness, and figure out together how to encourage each other to infuse the gospel into this week's regular rhythms. And remember, some of this – maybe most of this – can't be limited to the one "official" meeting of your community each week, and this discussion is simply acknowledging who you are personally, as a redeemed follower of Jesus, as you do life together.*

1. From this week's preparation for today's discussion, what stood out to you as you considered living out these identities and rhythms in your own life of discipleship?

2. From this week's personal preparation, is there anything you're confused by/have questions about? What was difficult to read/ponder?

3. Were there any questions, confusion, or concern that came up regarding Jesus's past, present, and future work in the gospel? (Day Two)

4. What ideas did we come up with regarding the family side of our discipleship? (Day Three) Are there a few things we can all commit to do for the coming months?

5. What ideas did we come up with regarding the servant side of our discipleship? (Day Four) Are there a few things we can all commit to do for the coming months?

6. What ideas did we come up with regarding the missionary side of our discipleship? (Day Five) Are there a few things we can all commit to do for the coming months?

7. Does anyone have any concerns with the plan we're making? If so, how can we address those concerns, with both a willingness to hear and consider the concern as valid, and also a willingness to press each other toward applying the gospel into it if needed?

8. Spend some time listening to God together. Ask him to reveal if there anything we've left out. If any thoughts come to mind, consider if they fit into the plan we're making.

9. Since this is your last meeting together, read "A Closing Note" on page 211 of this Field Guide. Then decide on next steps: does your community commit to carry out your plan together for the next year? Do you disband and start this process over, leading other groups? Something else? Whatever you decide, commit your plan to God, then celebrate communion together, remembering that all this stems from God, is meant to glorify God, and is completely reliant on God.

⊙ *Close your meeting in prayer.*

# REST

## WEEK 8, DAY 7

Every previous week has ended with a floating Day of Rest. You and your community have done a lot of work over the past eight weeks, so we encourage you to end your "Field Guide journey" with one final Day of Rest. Process and pray through what you've learned over the last eight weeks. Take stock of where you are personally and where the members of your group are. Maybe you feel like your journey into gospel saturation is just beginning, or maybe your community is deciding to take a break and ask the Spirit for clear direction before making any decisions . Maybe you're unsure or anxious about the next steps, and how the group's decisions will impact your life. Or maybe you're thrilled and excited—even over-eager!?—to take some big next steps.

Wherever you find yourself here at the tail end of this journey, it's right and good to end your eight weeks together, with one more Day of Rest. As you have every other week, use this day to intentionally stop. Slow down. Be still. Trust God. Admit you're *not* God! We reflect God's satisfaction in his own work when we pause and admit satisfaction in what we've accomplished (even if there's more to be done). And even more so, this day reminds us to be ultimately satisfied in Him. He is sufficient for our every need, we rely on His power and leading to accomplish anything good, we don't have to work to earn his approval, and He is in control regardless of our action or inaction.

# a closing note

In every moment when we are with others, the question isn't, "Are we sowing?" We are sowing seeds all of the time. And the question isn't, "Are we making disciples?" We are always making disciples. People are watching, learning, and listening to what we believe and how we live, and we are discipling them toward someone or something.

The question then is who or what are we discipling people toward. Away or toward Jesus? Jesus wants you to sow to the Spirit and experience eternal life. And he wants you to make disciples who will also experience eternal life.

Our prayer is that you will sow to the Spirit by seeking Jesus's glory in all of life. We pray too that you will learn to depend on the Spirit's strength rather than your own. We are convinced that if you do, you will be like the plants in a garden—dropping seeds wherever you go: gospel seeds in your home, at work, at the café, and along the path everywhere you walk. Those seeds you sow will, by the Spirit, produce more life and fruit, leading to more seeds sown.

That kind of seed-sowing leads to a movement from one life to the next and on to the ends of the earth. That's how God designed it to work when you:

- Surrender and devote yourself to Jesus.
- Remember and live in light of your new identity.
- Get on mission with a small group of people.

When God's people covenant together to sow gospel seeds in the everyday rhythms of life, a ripple effect moves through our lives, out toward the whole earth, saturating it with the good news of Jesus.

Whoever believes in me, as the Scripture has said, 'Out of his heart will flow rivers of living water.' JOHN 7:38

**This week isn't a conclusion—** ***this week is your commission!***

# Whats Next?
# A few recommendations after the *Saturate Field Guide*.

Gospel Fluency Handbook

Gospel Basics for Kids

Growing in Christ Together (Leader Guide)

Growing in Christ Together (Participant Guide)

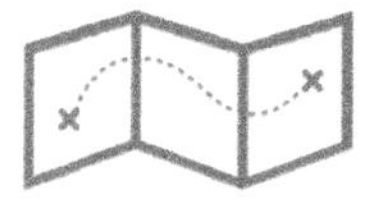

## Training
Events & Onsite.

## Coaching
Group coaching aimed at helping you plan, act and succeed in your calling.

## Resources
Videos, downloads, books and other tools to help you lead, teach and develop.

## Community
Join the conversation with access to experts and fellow disciple-makers.

## Consultations
Equip your church to make disciples in communities on mission.

## saturatetheworld.com

Leading Disciples of Jesus Toward Gospel Saturation

facebook.com/SaturateTheWorld

twitter.com/SaturateWorld

instagram.com/SaturateTheWorld

Made in the USA
Middletown, DE
23 July 2022